Cambridge Elements

Elements in Music and Musicians, 1750–1850
edited by
Simon P. Keefe
University of Sheffield

THE ORCHESTRA OF THE CAPPELLA REALE, NAPLES, 1750–1800

Anthony R. DelDonna
Georgetown University

Shaftesbury Road, Cambridge CB2 8EA, United Kingdom

One Liberty Plaza, 20th Floor, New York, NY 10006, USA

477 Williamstown Road, Port Melbourne, VIC 3207, Australia

314–321, 3rd Floor, Plot 3, Splendor Forum, Jasola District Centre, New Delhi – 110025, India

103 Penang Road, #05–06/07, Visioncrest Commercial, Singapore 238467

Cambridge University Press is part of Cambridge University Press & Assessment, a department of the University of Cambridge.

We share the University's mission to contribute to society through the pursuit of education, learning and research at the highest international levels of excellence.

www.cambridge.org
Information on this title: www.cambridge.org/9781009551083

DOI: 10.1017/9781009551090

© Anthony R. DelDonna 2025

This publication is in copyright. Subject to statutory exception and to the provisions of relevant collective licensing agreements, no reproduction of any part may take place without the written permission of Cambridge University Press & Assessment.

When citing this work, please include a reference to the DOI 10.1017/9781009551090

First published 2025

A catalogue record for this publication is available from the British Library

ISBN 978-1-009-55108-3 Hardback
ISBN 978-1-009-55107-6 Paperback
ISSN 2732-558X (online)
ISSN 2732-5571 (print)

Cambridge University Press & Assessment has no responsibility for the persistence or accuracy of URLs for external or third-party internet websites referred to in this publication and does not guarantee that any content on such websites is, or will remain, accurate or appropriate.

The Orchestra of the Cappella Reale, Naples, 1750–1800

Elements in Music and Musicians, 1750–1850

DOI: 10.1017/9781009551090
First published online: March 2025

Anthony R. DelDonna
Georgetown University

Author for correspondence: Anthony R. DelDonna, deldonna@georgetown.edu

Abstract: The most prestigious musical ensemble of early-modern Naples remained the Royal Chapel or Cappella Reale di Palazzo. Conceived to serve directly the ruling authority of the capital city – whether the viceroy (Spanish or Austrian) or monarchs (Carlo di Borbone then Ferdinando) – membership in this elite organization offered prestige, financial security, and access to the broader networks of music culture in Naples, attracting the best musicians within and beyond the physical confines of the capital. This Element introduces readers to the largely unknown history of the Neapolitan Cappella Reale in the second half of the eighteenth century. It is based on primary sources, reconstructing the entire personnel of the ensemble (1750–99), recovering previously unstudied contractual agreements, offering details about the musicians while also examining the original music of the principal musicians of the orchestra.

Keywords: Naples, eighteenth century, Cappella Reale, instrumental music, orchestras

© Anthony R. DelDonna 2025

ISBNs: 9781009551083 (HB), 9781009551076 (PB), 9781009551090 (OC)
ISSNs: 2732-558X (online), 2732-5571 (print)

Contents

1 History, Context, and Neapolitan Court Life   1

2 Operations, Organizational Structure, Formation, and Personnel   26

3 *Maestri-Operisti/Maestri-Strumentisti*   61

Bibliography   89

1 History, Context, and Neapolitan Court Life[1]

The most prestigious musical ensemble of early-modern Naples remained the Royal Chapel or, as it has been more precisely referenced, the Cappella Reale di Palazzo.[2] Conceived to serve directly the ruling authority of the capital city – whether the viceroy (Spanish or Austrian) or monarch (Carlo di Borbone, then his son and heir Ferdinando), membership in this elite organization represented the "seal of a specialized craft, goal of a 'ladder of advancement' means by which to attain a legal, financial, [and] professional status."[3] Membership in the Cappella Reale offered prestige, financial security, and access to the broader networks of music culture in Naples, attracting the best musicians within and beyond the physical confines of the capital. Similar to the metaphorical allusions to power of stage drama, encomiastic cantatas performed before operas, and displays of grandeur within the myriad *feste* sponsored by the court, the Cappella Reale existed to underline demonstrations of authority and sovereignty. This core mission often took the guise of inward-facing events (private celebrations and/or performances) as well as public displays including religious processions, civic ceremonies, and visits of foreign dignitaries. The Cappella Reale also maintained an intimate rapport with ecclesiastical authorities and establishments, above all the Cappellano Maggiore and the primary churches of the city as well as the archbishop for public events in the Cathedral of San Gennaro. Management of the ensemble remained in tune with the liturgical calendar of the church, often imparting a carefully curated political ideology

---

[1] This Element reflects the first stage of a monograph currently in course of creation and focused on the Cappella Reale, its activities and musicians during the Bourbon reign (1734–1800).

[2] See Guido Olivieri, *String Virtuosi in Eighteenth-Century Naples: Culture, Power, and Music Institutions* (Cambridge: Cambridge University Press, 2024); Guido Olivieri, "La musica strumentale a Napoli." in Francesco Cotticelli and Paologiovanni Maione, eds., *Storia della musica e dello spettacolo a Napoli: Il Seicento* (Naples: Turchini edizioni, 2020), 1493–1535; Guido Olivieri, "Condizione sociale dei musicisti nella Napoli del '700," in Pierpaolo DeMartino, ed., *Napoli Musicalissima: Studi in onore del 70.mo compleanno di Renato Di Benedetto* (Lucca: LIM, 2006), 45–68; Guido Olivieri, *Marchitelli, Mascitti e la musica strumentale napoletana fra Sei e Settecento* (Lucca: LIM, 2023); Francesco Cotticelli and Paologiovanni Maione, *Onesto divertimento ed allegria de' popoli: Materiali per una storia dello spettacolo a Napoli nel primo Settecento* (Milan: Ricordi, 1996); Francesco Cotticelli and Paologiovanni Maione, eds., *Storia della musica e dello spettacolo a Napoli: Il Settecento* (Naples: Turchini edizioni, 2009); Francesco Cotticelli and Paologiovanni Maione, eds., *Le istituzioni musicali a Napoli durante il vicaregno austriaco (1707–1734): Materiali inediti sulla Real Cappella ed il Teatro di S. Bartolomeo* (Naples: Luciano editore, 1993); Ulisse Prota-Giurleo, "Breve storia del Teatro di Corte e della musica a Napoli nei secoli XVII–XVIII." In Felice De Filippis and Ulisse Prota-Giurleo, eds., *Il Teatro di Corte del Palazzo Reale di Napoli* (Naples: L'Arte Tipografica, 1952), 19–146; Ulisse Prota-Giurleo, *I teatri di Napoli nel secolo XVII*, ed. Ermanno Bellucci and Giorgio Mancini, 3 vols. (Naples: Il quartiere, 2002); Anthony R. DelDonna, *Instrumental Music in Late Eighteenth-Century Naples: Politics, Patronage and Artistic Culture* (Cambridge: Cambridge University Press, 2021).

[3] Cotticelli and Maione, *Le istituzioni musicali a Napoli*, 8.

to the sacred sphere. Given the group's prominent political placement and religious, social, and artistic standing, a series of enduring and densely intertwined administrative and organizational mechanisms emerged between the prevailing temporal authority (Spanish, Austrian, or Bourbon) and the ensemble as well as vested stakeholders such as the Catholic Church. These structures remained stable throughout the early modern period, especially during the eighteenth century. Nevertheless, select and often fundamental elements of organization, and even more importantly taste and direction, remained within the purview of the ruling establishment and were often imposed unilaterally by such temporal powers.[4]

The Birth of the *Regno di Napoli*

The present inquiry focuses on the Cappella Reale during the initiation and long reign of the Bourbon dynasty, namely Carlo di Borbone (r. 1734–59) and his heir Ferdinando (r. 1759–98; 1799–1806; 1815–16).[5] In particular, it places the focus on the second half of the eighteenth century (1750–1800), a time which has been characterized as an *età d'oro* (or "golden age"), occasioned by political stability and peace, economic prosperity, a rising profile within continental affairs, and above all, artistic, especially musical, excellence. The renown of Naples as a capital of music took flight in the prior century, and by the time that the eighteen-year-old Carlo di Borbone ascended the throne of the newly established and independent kingdom in 1734, musical practices had already achieved European renown.[6] Nevertheless, fundamental questions remain about the continued artistic, political, and social roles of the Cappella Reale as well as its enduring constitution, membership, and artistic responsibilities in the second half of the eighteenth century. Of particular interest is how Carlo di Borbone (and his range of advisors) maintained continuity to, or selectively jettisoned past administrative structures and policies (of his Spanish and Austrian predecessors) to suit not only his myriad agendas, but also the highest artistic standards. In addition, a consideration of how the founding of the orchestra of the Teatro di San Carlo (1737), newly established in the early years of Carlo's reign, impacted the operation and status of the ensemble as well as its membership. Following Carlo's departure

---

[4] Olivieri, *String Virtuosi in Eighteenth-Century Naples*, 25.
[5] See Giuseppe Galasso and Rosario Romeo, eds., *Storia del Mezzogiorno*, 15 vols. (Naples: Edizioni del Sole, 1991–); Giuseppe Galasso, ed., *Storia del Regno di Napoli*, 6 vols. (Turin: UTET, 2006); Tommaso Astarita, *Between Salt Water and Holy Water: A History of Southern Italy* (New York: W. W. Norton & Co., 2006).
[6] See Francesco Cotticelli and Paologiovanni Maione, eds., *Storia della musica: Il Seicento*, (Naples: Turchini edizioni, 2020) and *Storia della musica: Il Settecento*.

for Madrid to inherit the Spanish throne,[7] the Neapolitan Kingdom entered a period of regency (1759–67), which hosted the transition to Ferdinand's rule. Scant attention has been given to this episode in the history of the Cappella Reale, and one scholar has indeed asserted that the ensemble all but ceased to exist during this phase of manifest change within Neapolitan political life and culture.

The broad span of Bourbon rule in the eighteenth century witnessed significant change and marked differences in philosophy, priorities, and orientation between father and son. Nevertheless, the foundation of the independent monarchy addressed the longstanding, inherent issues of foreign rule from afar and evident liabilities of appointing a viceroy. Carlo di Borbone immediately centralized power in the capital city and transparently challenged the autonomy of the vast feudal institutions as well as barons in the surrounding *paesi* that had exercised substantial sway over economic affairs.[8] The extensive moral, social, and financial influence of the Catholic Church, its vast network among local institutions and nobility (local and foreign, especially Carlo's mother Elisabetta Farnese) and dispensation from taxation presented complex considerations for the crown and its advisors. These competing forces, both internal and external, endured throughout the century and, for both Carlo and Ferdinando, they remained inherently linked. An evident continuity between their respective tenures emerges in the expressed objective to consolidate then extend the independence of the kingdom, to modernize the physical, political, and social infrastructures, and to affirm then assert Naples as a principal stakeholder in European affairs. The latter coincided with the expansion of commerce and trade as well as the building of a naval fleet and professional army. In regard to local affairs, there were significant challenges to the fiscal freedoms long accorded to the church and the feudal barons. In particular, both father and son reduced the financial privileges (marked by a highly controversial suspension of the *Chinea*)[9] and authorized the expulsion of the Jesuits. The Bourbons

---

[7] See Pietro Napoli Signorelli, *Vicende della cultura delle Due Sicile*, vol. 7 (Naples: Vincenzo Flauto, 1811), 3; Mirella Mafrici, *Il re delle speranze: Carlo di Borbone da Madrid a Napoli* (Naples: Edizioni scientifice italiane, 1998); Giuseppe Caridi, *Essere re e non essere re: Carlo di Borbone a Napoli e le attese deluse 1737–1738* (Soveria Mannelli: Rubbettino, 2006); Rosa Mincuzzi, ed., *Lettere di Bernardo Tanucci a Carlo III di Borbone (1759–1776)* (Rome: Istituto per la storia del Risorgimento italiano, 1969); Luigi Barreca, *Il tramonto di Bernardo Tanucci nella corrispondenza con Carlo III di Spagna, 1776–1783* (Palermo: U. Manfredi, 1976).

[8] Girolamo Imbruglia, ed., *Naples in the Eighteenth Century: The Birth and Death of a Nation State* (Cambridge: Cambridge University Press, 2000); in particular Giovanni Montroni, "The Court: Power and Social Life," 22–43; Maria Grazia Maiorini, "The Capital and Provinces," 4–22.

[9] See Girolamo Lioy, "L'abolizione della Chinea," *Archivio storico per le province napoletane*, Anno VII – Fascicoli I–IV (Naples: Vavaliere Francesco Giannini 1882), 263–292; 497–530; 713–775.

reduced the jurisdictional reach of the feudal barons, in favor of fostering entrepreneurial systems and even founded the silk colony of San Leucio, which promoted individual and equal rights.[10] The longstanding and broad-based collaboration with local intellectuals bore significant results for cultural reforms. Advisors such as the Count of Santo Stefano, Marchese Montealegre, Bernardo Tanucci, Celestino Galiani, Gaetano Filangieri, and Antonio Genovesi (to name only a select few) were attuned to modern, contemporary society as well as progress. Within their respective sectors of expertise, they engaged in constructing systems beneficial to the kingdom, designed to achieve the initiatives of Carlo and Ferdinando, albeit transparently grounded in Anglo-French "enlightened despotism." One evident outcome occurred in 1752, when the University of Naples, Federico II became the first institution in Europe to establish a chair in economics and commerce, occupied by Genovesi. The physical transformation of the capital and immediately adjacent areas remained a priority beginning with the expansion of the Palazzo Reale, the construction of the Teatro di San Carlo, as well as the residences of Portici, Capodimonte, and Caserta. The rediscovery of Pompeii and Herculaneum fueled tourism and the visits of foreign intellectuals undertaking the Grand Tour.[11] Their respective dynastic marriages also imparted tangible impacts, albeit differing in political, social, and artistic outcomes, for Carlo and Ferdinando. The arrival of Maria Amalia in 1738 marked a period of cohesion in which past traditions of mere representation became transformed into concrete acts. For Ferdinando, his long union to Maria Carolina proved to be politically disastrous, but also occasioned an unprecedented and sustained phase of broad artistic patronage.[12]

---

[10] See Nadia Verdile, "Maria Carolina e la Colonia di San Leucio," in Mirella Mafrici, ed., *All'ombra della corte*, (Naples: Friderciana Editrice Universitaria, 2010), 83–95; Nadia Verdile, *L'utopia di Carolina: Il codice delle leggi leuciane* (Naples: Regione Campania, 2007).

[11] See DelDonna, *Instrumental Music in Late Eighteenth-Century Naples*, 1–10; Cesare De Seta, "Grand Tour: The Lure of Italy in the Eighteenth Century" in Andrew Wilton and Ilaria Bignamini, eds., *Grand Tour: The Lure of Italy in the Eighteenth Century* (London: Tate Gallery Publishing, 1996), 13–19; Johann Wolfgang van Goethe, *I miei giorni a Napoli* (Naples: Edizioni Libreria Dante & Descartes, 2016).

[12] See essays in Giulio Sodano and Giulio Brevetti, eds., *Io, la regina: Maria Carolina d'Asburgo-Lorena tra politica, fede, arte e cultura*, Quaderni 33 (Palermo: Mediterranea – ricerche storiche 2016); Cinzia Recca, ed., *The Diary of Queen Maria Carolina of Naples, 1781–1785: New Evidence of Queenship at Court* (Basingstoke: Palgrave Macmillan, 2017); Mafrici, *All'ombra della corte*; Raffaele Ajello, "I filosofi e la regina: il governo delle Due Sicilie da Tanucci a Caracciolo (1776–1786)," *Rivista Storica Italiana* 13 (1991): 398–454, 657–738; Giovanni Astuto, "Dalle riforme alle rivoluzioni: Maria Carolina d'Asburgo: una regina austriaca nel Regno di Napoli e di Sicilia," *Quaderni del Dipartimento di Studi Politici* 1 (2007): 27–51.

An Emblem of Power and Musical Excellence

For Carlo di Borbone, the Palazzo Reale became the gravitational center of the city and by extension of the kingdom itself, at whose foundation remained the "material spaces of the palace, theater, and *cappella*."[13] These physical areas created a synergy, providing crucial and longstanding continuity among ceremonial, artistic, and religious spheres of interest, policy, and governance. At the center of these activities and initiatives promulgated by the court (as well as their intrinsic functions) remained the ensemble and musicians of the Cappella Reale. In the early years of his reign, Carlo preserved continuity to administrative mechanisms and artistic standards established by both his Spanish and Austrian predecessors. In addition, he had inherited a Cappella whose personnel had been largely assembled by Alessandro Scarlatti and Francesco Mancini.[14] Nevertheless, he did not hesitate either to impart change or to express dissatisfaction when issues occurred with the ensembles.[15] Insights into Carlo's engagement with the Cappella are expressed within surviving materials spanning diverse *fondi* in the Archivio di Stato di Napoli.[16] The correlation of such documents provides detailed insights into the administrative policies of governance, compensation, and personnel, often intersecting with professional standards, values, and the larger purposes of the ensemble. For the musicians of the Cappella Reale, many of the past frameworks remained in place. Providing leadership (both artistic and often administrative) at the head of the Cappella remained the *primo maestro* and his second the *vice-maestro*. The ensemble continued, moreover, to be organized according to regular "Plans" (referenced as either *pianta* or *planta*) noting the specific constitution of voices and instruments. Ordinary members held a *piazza* awarded either through a *concorso* (e.g. public competition) or direct appointment by officials, signifying their full-time, permanent status, while part-time members or supernumeraries were often times unpaid and longstanding adjunct musicians. The latter served as substitutes for missing members, often for reasons of health or specific needs of the ensemble. The passage from unpaid

---

[13] Maione, *Le istituzioni musicali a Napoli*, 26–36; Prota-Giurleo "Breve storia del Teatro di Corte," 110–113.

[14] See Ralf Krause, "Documenti per la storia della Real Cappella di Napoli nella prima metà del Settecento," *Annali dell'Istituto italiano per gli studi storici* 11 (1993): 235–257; Ralf Krause, "Das musikalische Panorama am neapolitanischen Hofe: zur Real Cappella di Napoli im frühen 18. Jahrhundert," *Analecta Musicologica* 30 (1998): 271–293.

[15] See Maione, *Le istituzioni musicali a Napoli*, 26–30.

[16] Archivio di Stato di Napoli, Fondo *Cappellanno Maggiore* (select volumes), *Casa reale antica* 343 II B *categorie diverse, Ministero degli affari ecclesiastici* and *Tesoreria antica Scrivania di Razione e Ruota dei Conti* (select volumes).

supernumerary to ordinary status did occur, but involved a lengthy, frequently unguaranteed process that occurred only when a position was rendered available, customarily through the death of a full-time member. The aforementioned organizational norms can be extrapolated from a range of primary archival sources. Table 1 presents the *organico* for the Cappella Reale from 1737, which also coincides (later in the year) with the inauguration of the Teatro di San Carlo.[17]

The mere existence of this register confirms, as asserted elsewhere, that Carlo di Borbone had indeed mandated a detailed accounting of musicians each month and, as such, verification of their continuous engagement within the ensemble. This roster provides no more than the month of service, followed by the entire listing of members and a declaration of accuracy. This affirmation specifies, "I the undersigned with trustworthiness as First Governor and Treasurer of the Monte of Musicians of the Royal Chapel of the Royal Palace [declare] that in the past month of April of the current year 1737 that the underwritten *virtuosi* have served with complete compliance in all events occurring in said Royal Chapel and such musicians are as noted."[18] Differing from a *pianta*, it does not provide the specific role, compensation, or status (as ordinary or supernumerary) for the musicians listed. Nevertheless, it does confirm that in 1737, the Cappella consisted of fifty-two members led by Mancini and Domenico Sarro as *primo* and *vice-maestro* respectively. More importantly, it reveals that under Bourbon rule, the Cappella continued to be conceptualized as four "choirs" embodying four distinct components: voices (soprano, alto, tenor, and bass, with a clear emphasis on the soprano), strings (violins, violas, cellos, and basses), winds (oboe and bassoon), and brass (*corni da caccia* and trumpets).[19] The musicians that performed on the aforementioned wind and brass instruments undoubtedly doubled when necessary. The presence of the bassoon section (led by long-term member Salvatore Lizio) typically took its place as part of the continuo group. Taken altogether, this folio (and those that follow) confirm that the Bourbon court had retained the organization of the ensemble as had been expressed in earlier *piante* crafted by either the Spanish or Austrian administrations.[20]

---

[17] Archivio di Stato di Napoli, *Casa reale antica* 343 II B *categorie diverse*.
[18] *Casa reale antica* 343 II B *categorie diverse*, folio 1r.
[19] The present folio omits the names of brass instrumentalists; however, this likely signifies supernumerary status. Piano and de Muro initiate their longstanding service to the Cappella in the rosters that follow this document.
[20] See Olivieri, *String virtuosi*, Krause, "Documenti per la storia della Real Cappella di Napoli" and Maione, *Le istituzioni musicali a Napoli*.

Table 1 Cappella Reale di Napoli, 1737

Name	Role
Francesco Mancini	Primo Maestro di Cappella
Domenico Sarro	Vice-Maestro di Cappella
Matteo Sassoni	Soprano
Domenico Gizzi	Soprano
Gaetano Majorano (Caffarelli)	Soprano
Nicola Ricchetti	Soprano
D. Francesco Guardia	Soprano
Domenico Melchiorre	Contralto
Pietro Giordano	Contralto
D. Nicodemo Nicolai	Contralto
Francesco Alarcon	Contralto
Tommaso Scarlatti	Tenor
D. Alessandro Inguscio	Tenor
Diego Natoli	Tenor
Lorenzo Baldacchini	Tenor
D. Francesco Caffarano	Bass
Giovanni Battista Palomba	Bass
Gioacchino Corrado	Bass
Geronimo Piano	Bass
Nicola Alborea	Violin
Carlo Giardino	Violin
Giuseppe Avitrano	Violin
Giuseppe Salernitano	Violin
Giacomo Vittozzi	Violin/Cello
Antonio Infantes	Violin
Domenico de Matteis	Violin
Giovanni Sebastiano	Violin
Domenico Salernitano	Violin
Vito Antonio Pagliarulo	Violin
Carlo Antonio Giannassi	Violin
Crescenzo Pepe	Violin
Francesco Supriani	Cello
Francesco Aversano	Contrabass
Gioacchino Bruno	Contrabass
Gaetano Besozzi	Oboe
Giuseppe Besozzi	Oboe
Giovanni Comes	Oboe

Table 1 (cont.)

Name	Role
Salvatore Lizio	Bassoon
Filippo Brandi	Bassoon
Paolo Pierro	Bassoon/Oboe
Nicola Ugolino	Lute
Matteo Sarao	Lute
Salvatore Toto	Lute
Leonardo Leo	First organist
Pietro Scarlattti	Organist
Giuseppe Vitigliano	Organist
Giovanni Veneziano	Organist
Giuseppe de Bottis	Organist
Andrea Basso	Organist
Antonio Raicola	Organist
Tommaso de Martino	Organaro

Table 2 Cappella Reale di Napoli, 1750

Name	Role
Giuseppe di Majo	Primo Maestro di Cappella
D. Giuseppe Marchitti	Vice-Maestro di Cappella
Domenico Gizzi	Soprano
Gaetano Majorano (Caffarelli)	Soprano
Giovanni Manzuoli	Soprano
Giuseppe Passari	Soprano
Nicola Ricchetti	Soprano
D. Francesco Guardia	Soprano
Francesco Bilancione	Treble
Biaggio Bisucci	Treble
Giovanni Tedeschi Amadori	Contralto
D. Nicodemo Nicolai	Contralto
Francesco Alarcon	Contralto
Gennaro de Magistris	Tenor
Francesco Tolve	Tenor
Gregorio Babbi	Tenor
Tommaso Scarlatti	Tenor
D. Alessandro Inguscio	Tenor

Table 2 (cont.)

Name	Role
D. Michele Forni	Bass
D. Francesco Caffarano	Bass
Giovanni Battista Palomba	Bass
Geronimo Piano	Bass
Carlo Giardino	Violin
Giuseppe Avitrano	Violin
Giuseppe Salernitano	Violin
Giacomo Vittozzi	Violin/Cello
Antonio Infantes	Violin
Domenico de Matteis	Violin
Nicola Fiorenza	Violin
Saverio Carcais	Violin
Francesco Paciotti	Violin
Crescenzo Pepe	Violin
Costantino Roberto	Violin
Nicola Fabio	Violin
Aniello Santangelo	Violin
Gaetano Salernitano	Violin
Giuseppe Romano	Violin
Francesco Supriani	Cello
Francesco Giampriano	Cello
Gioacchino Bruno	Contrabass
Andrea de Florio	Contrabass
Giovanni Comes	Oboe
Gaetano Besozzi	Oboe
Giuseppe Besozzi	Oboe
Ferdinando Lizio	Bassoon
Salvatore Lizio	Bassoon
Giovanni de Muro	Tromba
Nicola Ugolino	Lute
Matteo Sarao	Lute
Giuseppe de Bottis	Maestro di cappella soprannumerario
Giuseppe Vitigliano	Organist
Domenico Merola	First Organist
GianFrancesco di Majo	Organist
Tommaso de Martino	Organaro

By 1750 and continuing further into Carlo's reign, these folios reveal that the Cappella Reale sustained constant change, not simply replacing older members but also demonstrating a clear awareness and sensitivity to internal balance and practical needs. Table 2 presents the *organico* from January 1750,[21] noting a slight expansion in numbers within the ensemble (fifty-three in total, albeit with two noted as absent).

Even more noteworthy is that the core of the ensemble remained consistent with twenty-eight members from 1737 still active in the Cappella. There had also been a change in leadership with Giuseppe di Majo serving as *primo maestro* and Giuseppe Marchitti as *vice-maestro*.[22] Two of the most famous castrato voices of the eighteenth century continued to serve the Cappella, namely Domenico Gizzi and Gaetano Majorano, the latter better known by his stage name of "Caffarelli."[23] The ensemble displays consistent numbers of strings (albeit some noted as "violin" undoubtedly played viola), winds, and brass. Although these data provide basic statistics and demonstrate continuity in the ensemble, it is in correlative primary sources that specifics emerge about administrative policies. In particular, volumes within the Fondo *Ministero degli affari ecclesiastici*, emanating from the office of the Cappellano Maggiore, contain a broad array of information. For example, even prior to di Majo's ascension, one entry from 1742 reads:

> In light of the death of Domenico Salernitano, who served as violinist in the Royal Chapel with the compensation of 7 ducats per month, having recourse to the King with the appended eleven supplications by different petitioners for his position; And by order of His Majesty, they are provided to [Your Royal Majesty] in order to receive from the Maestro di Cappella Domenico Sarro who will inform us with his opinion whether it is necessary to replace this position of violin with a vocalist, or another instrument, or [whether] it is superfluous [and] therefore to delete it. . . . Royal Palace 29 April 1742.[24]

This entry highlights Salernitano's generous compensation,[25] while also outlining that a noteworthy eleven supplicants had requested his position within the ensemble. Even more interesting is that the *primo maestro* Sarro had been

---

[21] *Casa reale antica* 343 II B *categorie diverse*, f. 148v.

[22] See *Tesoreria antica*, # 67, f. 29 and 30r respectively.

[23] See Martha Feldman, *The Castrato: Reflections on Natures and Kinds* (Berkeley: University of California Press, 2016); Winton Dean, "Caffarelli [Cafariello, Cafarellino, Gaffarello]," *Grove Music Online*. 2001; Accessed June 11, 2024. www.oxfordmusiconline.com/grovemusic/view/10.1093/gmo/9781561592630.001.0001/omo-9781561592630-e-0000004540.

[24] Archivio di Stato di Napoli; Fondo *Ministero degli affari ecclesiastici*, vol. 39; f. 61v.

[25] The standard currency and denomination for the Kingdom of Naples was the ducat (ducato). A single ducat could be divided into 5 tarì, further into 10 carlini, and finally into 100 grana. These currencies were replaced in the nineteenth century by the national standard of the lira. Allowing for inflation and cost-of-living adjustments, a single ducat from 1770 was equivalent to 4.37 lire in 1860, 10,472 lire in 1988, and 42,900 lire in 2000. The conversion to the euro currency in Italy occurred in 1999; the subsequent exchange rate was imposed as 1 euro equaling

consulted as to whether Salernitano's *piazza* should be assigned to another violinist or vocalist (by custom via *concorso*) or whether the post had become superfluous. The artistic authority of the *primo maestro* is clearly articulated in this process, while also underlining a pragmatism about the evolving needs of the ensemble; namely, whether another instrument, whose type is not specified, or voice, will best address prevailing requirements. This entry also initiated a series of subsequent comments documenting the varied deliberations and stakeholders involved in the replacement of Salernitano. The next entry (within the same volume of the *Ministero*) notes,

> I present for the consideration of Your Supreme Highness the two appended supplications, one of Gaetano Salernitano, and the other of Antonio Infantes, in which they request to be conferred the position of violinist which was vacated in the Royal Chapel due to the death of Domenico Salernitano ... Dios Gratia. Palazzo the 29th of April 1742. Marchese Brancaccio.[26]

By the time of this entry, the number of candidates appeared to have narrowed to the son of Salernitano (Gaetano) and Antonio Infantes, both of whom would be admitted to the Cappella. This supplication raises immediate questions: whether a *concorso* had been organized, the prior service of these musicians as supernumeraries, and the potential role of nepotism? It is also evident from these materials that newly admitted musicians did not receive the same level of compensation as the decedents. This may have been a strategy to reallocate funds by the administration of the Cappella to raise the salaries and retain key members of the ensemble, especially instrumentalists, who made notably less than their vocal counterparts. It may also have been a manner of imposing a probationary period upon the newly admitted musicians too. Nevertheless, and once again in the aftermath of the death of Salernitano, there is record that:

> Due to the death of Domenico Salernitano who has vacated the salary of seven ducats per month, which he enjoyed as a violinist in the Royal Chapel, and having determined to divide it in the manner as proposed by Your Excellency by means of the document dated the 9th of the present year, namely to Blas

---

1,936.27 lire. Therefore, 42,900 lire in 2000 convert to 22.16 euros in 2001, approximately 35 euros in 2004, and 31.61 euros in 2009. Based on the exchange rate in August 2024, 35.56 euros are the equivalent of 38.41 USD. See Domenico DeMarco, "Per la storia dell'artigianato a Napoli: una ricca fonte documentale." In Francesco Balletta, ed., *L'artigianato in Campania ieri ed oggi* (Naples: Istituto italiano per la storia delle imprese, 1991), 107. See Takasi Yamada, "L'attività e la strategia di Gennaro Blanchi, impresario dei teatri napoletani nella seconda metà del Settecento: Interpretazione del suo sistema di gestione dalle scritture dell'Archivio Storico dell'Istituto Banco di Napoli-Fondazione." In *Quaderni dell'archivio storico* (Naples: Istituto Banco di Napoli Fondazione, 2004), 95–133.

[26] *Ministero degli affari ecclesiastici*, vol. 39, f. 67v.

> Bisucci, treble voice three ducats per month, to Giuseppe de Muro, and to Giuseppe Romano *trombe de caccia* one ducat per month to each, to Nicola Fiorenza, and to Saverio Carcais, who are the supernumerary violinists with the longest tenure in this Royal Chapel, one ducat to each per month.[27]

This carefully crafted statement on one hand affirms the longstanding hierarchy of compensation (with its favorable predilection toward vocalists) by virtue of Bisucci having received almost half of the funds, while his instrumental colleagues divide the remainder, receiving individually no more than a single ducat each per month. Nonetheless, it is significant and discerning that Fiorenza and Carcais have been cited for their long tenures as supernumeraries, justifying their receipt of an increase in salary as well as recognition of their value.

The role of *primo maestro* remained a crucial and highly prized position, given its status, authority, generous compensation, and position as interlocutor between the administration and musicians of the Cappella Reale. The death of Domenico Sarro in April 1744 initiated a lengthy process and search for his successor. Evidence of the deliberations emerges in the proceedings of the *Ministero degli affari ecclesiatici* as follows:

> By the orders of the King, I refer to Your Highness the eight appended supplications of different musicians who seek the employment as Maestro di Cappella of the Royal Chapel, and other [requests] for salary increases such that Your Highness will keep in mind the new plan most recently formulated of the Royal Chapel dated 6 July 1742.[28]

Once again, the death of an ordinary member within the ensemble initiated not only petitions for the specific position, but also salary increases by existing members as referenced in the cited record. This entry also refers to the recently revised *pianta* of the ensemble (from July 1742), which delineated not only current members, but also the division of voices and instruments.[29] In subsequent records (and documented in the same volume of the *Ministero*), there is a further discussion on the ongoing process of determining Sarro's replacement. It reads as follows:

> I refer to Your Highness by order of the King the three included supplications, the first by Don Rinaldo Broschi, another by Saverio Carcais, and the other by Blas Bisucci, in which they request the position of Maestro di Cappella of the Royal Chapel, which has been vacated due to the death of Domenico Sarro.[30]

---

[27] *Ministero degli affari ecclesiastici*, vol. 39, f. 102r.
[28] *Ministero degli affari ecclesiastici*, vol. 67, f. 88r.
[29] Krause, "Documenti per la storia della Real Cappella di Napoli," 256–260, and Maione, *Le istituzioni musicali a Napoli*, 26–30.
[30] *Ministero degli affari ecclesiastici*, vol. 67, f. 88r.

Broschi, the first supplicant, was the older brother of the famed castrato, and one would imagine given his limited reputation (beyond the aforementioned familial connection) remained an outlier for the position. Both Carcais and Bisucci were current members of the ensemble, the former a long-time violinist and the latter a treble vocalist. In terms of a compositional profile, there is no surviving evidence of music by either individual, rendering the possibility of appointment as virtually nil.[31] Nevertheless, the longstanding administrative mechanisms of the Cappella articulated that the standing *vice-maestro* would attain *primo* status, while the *primo organista* was also elevated to the second position in leadership. These practices are confirmed in a subsequent record, noting that:

> Regarding the death of the previously cited Domenico Sarro Maestro di Cappella of the Royal Chapel, the King has accorded this position to Leonardo Leo, who has served as vice-maestro of the same [ensemble]. ... In the same manner, His Majesty has accorded to Giuseppe di Majo, *primo organista*, the position of vice-maestro of the Royal Chapel.[32]

Leo had been a longstanding member of the Cappella, whose desire to ascend to its leadership, had been finally fulfilled. Tragically, he suffered a fatal stroke only nine months into his tenure and once again the position of *primo maestro* lay vacant. The subsequent *concorso*, ultimately won by di Majo and surprisingly with Giuseppe Marchitti as *vice-maestro*, initiated "a palace intrigue" by virtue of Maria Amalia's attempt to influence the outcome by signaling her preference for di Majo to her countryman and friend Johann Adolph Hasse, one of the four outside evaluators of the *concorso*.[33]

The ascent of Giuseppe di Majo (appointed in September 1745) ushered in a long period of stability for the Cappella Reale, which spanned the end of Carlo's reign, the Regency and the early stirrings related to Ferdinando's inheritance of the throne. This constancy derived not only from well-established policies and procedures, but also from an evident respect demonstrated towards members of the ensemble. In terms of the former, entries of recompense for di Majo note that his level of renumeration and associated benefits continued "to follow the new plan for music for this Royal Chapel from July 6, 1742."[34] This continuity ensured that key principles remained intact, in both essential and minor matters. The primary

---

[31] There was no evidence of any surviving compositions of either individual in the Neapolitan archives or any music located on Opac-SBN.

[32] *Ministero degli affari ecclesiastici*, vol. 67, f. 122r. See also Prota-Giurleo, *La grande orchestra*, 11–13.

[33] See Krause, "Documenti per la storia della Real Cappella di Napoli," 253; Prota-Giurleo, "Breve storia del Teatro di Corte," 120–121.

[34] *Tesoreria antica Scrivania di Razione e Ruota dei Conti*, vol. 38, f. 123r.

intention of the aforementioned plan continued to place emphasis on maintaining personnel and in turn addressing related musical needs. In terms of the rapport between the Cappella's administration and its members, there is an evident and ongoing sense of equanimity at work. For example, financial registers note,

> His Majesty by Royal Order of May 5, 1759 having determined by means of Royal Clemency, to concede to the Musico Tenor of the Royal Chapel Gregorio Babbi, who has requested, to be able to retire to live with his family in Cesena his native city, of the Pontifical State, with the continuance, and benefit of his salary of 30 ducats per month, which he earns, by means of his employment in said Royal Chapel.[35]

The retention of full salary by a retiring member of the Cappella Reale occurred with regular frequency and Babbi's successful petition represented the norm rather than an exception. The administration proved to be equally generous with family relations, often siblings and children of current members, who sought employment with the ensemble, in some cases under extenuating circumstances. One of the most interesting episodes unfolded within the Besozzi family of renowned wind players. A payment registry regarding Gaetano Besozzi details his employment history with the Cappella, recounting:

> His Majesty by Royal Order of July 20, 1736 registered by the Secretary of State, War and Navy, has resolved that the position of oboist of the Royal Chapel held by Antonio Besozzi pass to his brother Gaetano, and to him will be accorded the same salary enjoyed by the same Antonio.[36]

Although one could allege that this process had been animated by a clear sense of nepotism, the Besozzi family were renowned as *virtuosi* oboists. Roughly at the same time, the request of Giuseppe Besozzi also appears in the same volume of *Tesoreria*, detailing that:

> His Majesty by Royal Order of July 31, 1738, has deigned to grant, in regard to the indisposition of [his] blindness, which has afflicted the cited Giuseppe Besozzi, who cannot continue to serve in the role of oboist of said Royal Chapel, [the King] has deigned to concede to him retirement with the salary of ten ducats per month of the nineteen presently earned, and the position of oboist to Antonio Besozzi, his son.[37]

This compassionate concession of retirement with the lion's share of his salary intact extended to the appointment of Besozzi's son in his place. It underlined, moreover, a transparent esteem for the service and abilities of this family of musicians.

---

[35] *Tesoreria antica*, vol. 38, f. 132r.   [36] *Tesoreria antica*, vol. 38, ff. 133r–135v.
[37] *Tesoreria antica*, vol. 38, f. 149r–150v.

A New Theatrical Ideal

At the initiation of Carlo's reign, a broad program of urban and civic renewal occurred at an unprecedented pace. This process of revival stemmed from clear political objectives, notably the status of Naples as the capital of a newly established, independent state, one eager to be recognized as a continental stakeholder. The King's advisors prioritized the royal palace, directing significant resources to its renovation and expansion, which included the construction of a new, eponymous royal theater. Realized in an astonishing seven months, the Teatro di San Carlo cultivated *opera seria* exclusively and through these dramas projected metaphorical representations of Bourbon power, authority, and sovereignty. The establishment of the San Carlo also raised practical questions regarding personnel.[38] Specifically, whether the musicians of the Cappella Reale would be offered membership in the ensemble of the opera orchestra.[39] Prior to its construction, the Bourbon court had continued to stage operas primarily at the Teatro San Bartolomeo and the orchestra of that ensemble had also retained members of the Cappella.[40] Given that the San Carlo formed a physical adjunct to the royal palace and the opera orchestra would now be expanded, the understanding of shared personnel represents a salient inquiry.[41] In regard to these fundamental questions, the scholar Ulisse Prota-Giurleo stated plainly that the San Carlo inherited the musicians associated with its predecessor, implying that members of the Cappella would be included, yet "integrated by new and choice members."[42] Table 3 provides a snapshot of

---

[38] See Cotticelli and Maione, *Le istituzioni musicali a Napoli*, 41–51.

[39] See Croce, *I teatri di Napoli*, 2 vols.; Prota-Giurleo, *La grande orchestra del R. Teatro San Carlo* (Napoli, 1927); Cotticelli and Maione, *Onesto divertimento ed allegria de' popoli*; Cotticelli and Maione, eds., *Storia della musica: il Settecento*, 2 vols.; Gian Giacomo Stiffoni, "Il Teatro di San Carlo dal 1747 al 1753," in Paologiovanni Maione, ed., *Fonti d'archivio per la storia della musica e dello spettacolo a Napoli tra XVI e XVIII secolo* (Naples: Editoriale Scientifica, 2001), 271–374; in the same volume, Lucio Tufano, "L'orchestra del Teatro San Carlo nel 1780 e nel 1796," 449–476; Anthony R. DelDonna, "Behind the Scenes: The Musical Life and Organizational Structure of the San Carlo Opera Orchestra in Late 18th-Century Naples," 427–448; Anthony R. DelDonna, "Production Practices at the Teatro di San Carlo, Naples, in the Late 18th Century," *Early Music* 30, no. 3 (August 2002), 429–445.

[40] See Cotticelli and Maione, *Onesto divertimento* and *Le istituzioni musicali*.

[41] See Fausto Nicolini, "I banchi pubblici napoletani e i loro archivi," in *Bollettino dell'Archivio Storico del Banco di Napoli I* (1950): 1–36; Nicolini, *L'Archivio Storico del Banco di Napoli. Una fonte preziosa per la storia economica, sociale, artistica del Mezzo giorno d'Italia* (Naples: L'Arte Tipografica, 1972); Domenico DeMarco and Eduardo Nappi, "Nuovi documenti sulle origini e sui titoli del Banco di Napoli," in *Revue Internationale d'Histoire de la Banque* 30–31 (1985), 1–78; see also Cotticelli and Maione, "Le carte degli antichi banchi e il panorama musicale e teatrale della Napoli di primo Settecento," *Studi Pergolesiani Pergolesi Studies* 4 (2000): 1–129; Cotticelli and Maione, "Le carte degli antichi banchi e il panorama musicale e teatrale della Napoli di primo Settecento: 1732–1734," *Studi Pergolesiani Pergolesi Studies* 5 (2006): 21–51 (including the accompanying CD).

[42] Prota-Giurleo, *La grande orchestra del San Carlo*, 7.

Table 3 Comparison of Cappella Reale and Teatro di San Carlo ensembles, 1750

Cappella Reale, 1750	Teatro di San Carlo, 1750
Violins:	
Carlo Giardino	**Domenico de Matteis**
Giuseppe Avritano	Benedetto Breglia
Giuseppe Salernitano	Mattia del Rio
Antonio Infantes	Michele Guarino
Domenico de Matteis	**Francesco Paciotti**
Nicola Fiorenza	Nicola Amatrice
Saverio Carcais	Tommaso Barone
Francesco Paciotti	Francesco Biscaglia
Crecenzo Pepe	Carlo Camerino
Costantino Roberto	Saverio Capriola
Nicola Fabio	Carlo de Falco
Aniello Santangelo	Domenico de Micco
Gaetano Salernitano	**Nicola Fabio**
Giuseppe Romano	Giuseppe Magrino
	Giuseppe Romano
	Gennaro Rotunno
	Aniello Santangelo
	Nicolò Tedesco
	Giacomo Vittozzi
	Agostino Zaccaria
	Bartolomeo Arte
	Giacomo Bergantino
	Gaetano Carfagna
	Giuseppe Casale
	Ferdinando Germani
	Venanzio Rizzano
	Nicola Tombarelli
	Viola:
	Giuseppe Orgitano
	Aniello Recena
	Francesco Antonio Giannassi
	Domenico Conti
Cello:	
Giacomo Vittozzi	
Francesco Supriani	
Francesco Giampriano	**Francesco Giampriano**

Table 3 (cont.)

Cappella Reale, 1750	Teatro di San Carlo, 1750
Contrabass:	
Andrea de Florio	**Andrea de Florio**
	Francesco Persico
	Luca Silvato
	Ascanio Vaccola
	Domenico Fischetti
Oboe:	
Giuseppe Besozzi	Francesco Papa
Gaetano Besozzi	Cherubino Corena
Giovanni Comes	Girolamo di Donato
Bassoon:	
Salvatore Lizio	**Salvatore Lizio**
Ferdinando Lizio	**Ferdinando Lizio**
Tromba:	
Gennaro Piano	Cesare Biancone
Giuseppe de Muro	**Giuseppe de Muro**
	Gennaro Piano
	Giuseppe Romano
Lute:	
Nicola Ugolino	
Matteo Sarao	
Organ:	Cembalo:
Domenico Merola	Nicola Conforto
Gian Francesco di Majo	Antonio Palella

a single year (1750), well within the reign of Carlo, at a time when administrative policies and procedures had been fine-tuned for both the Cappella and the San Carlo.

A noteworthy thirteen members of the Cappella (out of the thirty listed) served in both ensembles. Although on the surface this may not appear significant given the size of the opera orchestra, the musicians from the Cappella engaged in key roles for this ensemble. In particular, the violin virtuoso Domenico de Matteis also served as *primo violino* at the San Carlo. He was joined by his colleagues Paciotti, Fabio, Santangelo, and Romano, all of whom would hold these dual positions for extended terms. This core of violinists undoubtedly provided a sense of continuity from one ensemble to the other as well as establishing an essential sound and texture. Francesco Giampriano shared the cello stand with Vittozzi in both groups and Andrea de Florio provided leadership for the large contingent of contrabasses in the opera orchestra. Both Salvatore and Ferdinando Lizio served each ensemble as bassoonists, while Piano[43] and de Muro also performed on the *tromba de caccia* in either group. Taken altogether, this essential nucleus of musicians between the leading ensembles of the capital ensured that high standards and a sense of internal continuity remained in place. There is also the question of whether the San Carlo became an avenue for a position within the Cappella Reale. Although there are no specific documentary materials, there is evidence of long-term connections in shared personnel between the ensembles in the eighteenth century suggesting this possibility. In reference to Table 3, one such example is the case of Carlo Camerino, who will ascend to leadership in both ensembles during his storied career in Naples, which spanned the better part of the second half of the century.

The *interregnum*

In his twenty-five years of rule, Carlo di Borbone and his advisors had imparted clear models of civic governance, policy, and procedure, which extended to the broad range of cultural and artistic affairs. In his research on the Cappella Reale, its *primi maestri* and *organisti*, the scholar Hanns-Bertold Dietz has asserted that the activities of the ensemble came to a virtual halt as the rule of Carlo waned and the Regency took full hold.[44] The existing and extensive evidence suggests otherwise, verified through the ongoing documentation of the ensemble in the form of monthly rosters and a significant body of meticulous, informative correlative materials noting that standards as well as policies remained intact. Table 4 distills the memberships of the Cappella Reale in the period 1750–68.

These data reveal that in the final decade of Carlo's reign and the transition to that of Ferdinando, the ensemble remained a consistent and stable entity characterized by the four sections of voices, a well-appointed string cohort, and the essential wind and brass. Their forces could also be supplemented by additional instruments provided by the large corps of supernumeraries eager to establish themselves and hopefully gain permanent, compensated entry to the Cappella Reale. Nevertheless, a closer study of surviving documents reveals the internal dynamics at work in the ensemble, especially the transparent mechanisms to balance the vocal and instrumental *virtuosi*.

The vocal *virtuosi* of the ensemble have long embodied the renown of the Cappella Reale in Naples. Famed castrati such as Caffarelli, Gizzi, and Amadori

---

[43] Prota-Giurleo erroneously listed Girolamo, not Gennaro.
[44] See Hanns-Bertold Dietz, "A Chronology of Maestri and Organisti at the Cappella Reale in Naples, 1745–1800," *Journal of the American Musicological Society* 25 (1972): 379–406; Dietz, "Instrumental Music at the Court of Ferdinand IV of Naples and Sicily and the Works of Vincenzo Orgitano," *International Journal of Musicology* 1 (1992): 99–126.

Table 4 Cappella Reale di Napoli, 1750–68

Name	Role	Years of service
Giuseppe di Majo	Primo Maestro di Cappella	1750–68
D. Giuseppe Marchitti	Vice-Maestro di Cappella	1750–68
Pasquale Cafaro	Primo Maestro di Cappella	1750–68
Domenico Gizzi	Soprano	1750–58 †
Gaetano Majorano (Caffarelli)	Soprano	1750–68
Giovanni Manzuoli	Soprano	1750–57
Giuseppe Passari	Soprano	1750–68
Nicola Ricchetti	Soprano	1750–53
D. Francesco Guardia	Soprano	1750–52 †
Antonio Mazziotti	Soprano	1762–68
Giacomo Catelini	Soprano	1753–55
Giuseppe Aprile	Soprano	1752–55
Salvatore Consorti	Soprano	1758–68
Francesco Bilancione	Treble	1750–68
Biaggio Bisucci	Treble	1750–68
Giuseppe Guerra	Treble	1763–68
Giovanni Tedeschi Amadori	Contralto	1750–68
D. Nicodemo Nicolai	Contralto	1750–64 †
Francesco Alarcon	Contralto	1750–61†
Antonio Catena	Contralto	1762–68
Leopoldo Maccozzi	Contralto	1764–68
Santi Barbieri	Contralto	1750–68
Gennaro de Magistris	Tenor	1750–68
Francesco Tolve	Tenor	1750–68
Gregorio Babbi	Tenor	1750–68 †
Tommaso Scarlatti	Tenor	1750–53
D. Alessandro Inguscio	Tenor	1750–58 †
Felippo Cappellaro	Tenor	1768
Letterio Ferrari	Tenor	1758–68
Luiggi Mattei	Tenor	1768
D. Michele Forni	Bass	1750–68
D. Francesco Caffarano	Bass	1750–66 †
Giovanni Battista Palomba	Bass	1750–53 †
Geronimo Piano	Bass	1750–56 †
Antonio Calogero	Bass	1757–68
Domenico Guglietti	Bass	1767–68
Francesco Magri	Bass	1767–68

Table 4 (cont.)

Name	Role	Years of service
Taddeo Pucci	Bass	1766–67
Carlo Giardino	Violin	1750–62 †
Giuseppe Avitrano	Violin	1750–56 †
Giuseppe Salernitano	Violin	1750–66
Giacomo Vittozzi	Violin/Cello	1750–68
Antonio Infantes	Violin	1750–56 †
Domenico de Matteis	Violin	1750–58 †
Nicola Fiorenza	Violin	1750–64
Saverio Carcais	Violin	1750–68
Francesco Paciotti	Violin	1750–61 †
Crescenzo Pepe	Violin	1750–68
Costantino Roberto	Violin	1750–68
Nicola Fabio	Violin	1750–68
Aniello Santangelo	Violin	1750–68
Gaetano Salernitano	Violin	1750–68
Giuseppe Romano	Violin	1750–53
Antonio Moresca	Violin	1758–68
Emanuelle Barbella	Violin	1756–68
Francesco Lecce	Violin	1761–68
Francesco Piscina	Violin	1766–68
Gennaro Romanelli	Violin	1750–64
Gennaro Valente	Violin	1761–68
Gioacchino Sabatino	Violin	1756–68
Pietro Antonacci	Violin	1761–68
Francesco Supriani	Cello	1750–53
Francesco Giampriano	Cello	1750–52
Giuseppe Valerio	Cello	1764–68
Gioacchino Bruno	Contrabass	1750–66 †
Andrea de Florio	Contrabass	1750–68
Giuseppe de Florio	Contrabass	1766–68
Pietro Burlo	Contrabass	1766–68
Giovanni Comes	Oboe	1750–56
Gaetano Besozzi	Oboe	1750–65
Giuseppe Besozzi	Oboe	1750–61
Geronimo de Donato	Oboe	1751–68
Giuseppe Maria LaBanchi	Oboe	1767–68
Ferdinando Lizio	Bassoon	1750–68

Table 4 (cont.)

Name	Role	Years of service
Salvatore Lizio	Bassoon	1750–51 †
Giovanni de Muro	Tromba	1750–54
Gennaro Piano	Tromba	1753–68
Baldassare La Barbiera	Tromba	1754–68
Nicola Ugolino	Lute	1750–53
Matteo Sarao	Lute	1750–56 †
Giacomo Pensa	Lute	1756–64 †
Vito Ugolino	Lute	1753–68
Giuseppe de Bottis	Maestro di cappella soprannumerario	1750–54 †
Giuseppe Vitigliano	Organist	1750–66 †
Domenico Merola	First Organist	1750–68
GianFrancesco di Majo	Organist	1750–68
Francesco Corbisiero	Organist	1768
Pietro Scarlatti	Organist	1750 †
Tommaso de Martino	Organaro	1750–51 †
Domenico Antonio Russo	Organaro	1761–68

Note: The dagger symbols in the table indicate the year of the member's death.

became intimately associated with the group and its activities. Early in the eighteenth century, the vocal corps of the Cappella had often been engaged by the Spanish and Austrian vice-regal establishments for performances in private or the Teatro San Bartolomeo, typically for stage dramas.[45] As Carlo di Borbone settled into his reign and with the creation of the royal theater in 1737, the vocal *virtuosi* of the Cappella remained, yet they were less frequently engaged for opera performances at court given the status and success of the San Carlo. Based on surviving materials, it appears that their primary engagements related to religious occasions, often the principal holy days of the annual liturgical calendar. These events have been preserved in the *Gazzetta di Napoli* and provide a notable level of detail.[46] For example, in June 1735, the *Gazzetta* noted "in occasion of the octave of Corpus Domini, there were many processions held in the city . . .; [The one to San Giacomo] featured the participation of the Cappella

---

[45] Cotticelli and Maione, *Le istituzioni musicali a Napoli*; Benedetto Croce, *I teatri di Napoli*, 2 vols. (Naples: Berisio, 1968).
[46] Ausilia Magaudda and Danilo Costantini, *Musica e spettacolo nel Regno di Napoli attraverso lo spoglio della Gazzetta 1675–1768* (Rome: Ismez, 2009).

Reale of the court."⁴⁷ Three years later, once again for the Feast of Corpus Domini, the *Gazzetta* published a similar account of more extensive celebrations involving the collaboration "of the musicians and clergy of the Cappella Reale ... they performed the solemn *Te Deum*."⁴⁸ At times, the *Gazzetta* even notes specific identities and musical details about the Cappella. In 1740, it recounts that "there was organized a chapel ... with choice music, featuring string instruments and winds, the soprano Francesco Bilancione of His Majesty's Royal Chapel also performed."⁴⁹ Carlo and his spouse Maria Amalia had maintained a devout and conservative rapport with the church throughout their reign, embodied by the engagement of the Cappella for religious services. In the course of their rule, based on such evidence, it is apparent that the Cappella had increasingly been reserved for this type of regular service, albeit intermittent function. As such, it undoubtedly impacted the roles and activities of the vocal *virtuosi*. Confirmation of this assertion can be found in financial ledgers related to the Cappella. In 1754, records reveal that,

> His Majesty by means of Royal Order of August 24, 1754 deigns to grant the musician of the Royal Chapel Gaetano Majorano Caffarelli Royal Permission to be able to transfer to the Royal Court of Portugal, in order to serve in the role of soprano, according him as well the grace of continuing his salary that he earns as a musician of this Royal Chapel during his absence.

Caffarelli's counterpart and equally famed contralto Giovanni Tedeschi Amadori unfortunately had not been the beneficiary of the King's generosity. Specifically,

> His Majesty concedes ... to the musician of the Royal Chapel Giovanni Tedeschi Amadori His Royal Permission to travel in the coming month of October to perform in the theater of Alexandria [called the] *de la Palla* and to the same in the coming *Carnevale* in the theater of Milan with the condition that he must return to this city [Naples] for the coming Holy Week and commands that the continuation of salary be suspended to the aforementioned musician Giovanni Tedeschi Amadori.⁵⁰

Despite such difference in treatment, Amadori remained a valued asset and indeed embedded within these same entries are indications of keeping his salary in line with that of Caffarelli. With the passing of their famed colleague, the soprano Domenico Gizzi, documents outline a careful raising of each virtuoso's salary, detailing that "having been vacated given the death of the Soprano Domenico Gizzio [sic], [it has been decided to] raise the salary of Caffarelli

---

⁴⁷ Magaudda and Costantini, *Musica e spettacolo*, 497.
⁴⁸ Magaudda and Costantini, *Musica e spettacolo*, 567.
⁴⁹ Magaudda and Costantini, *Musica e spettacolo*, 614.   ⁵⁰ *Tesoreria antica*, # 38; f. 129r.

by five ducats over the present thirty that he obtains, for a total of thirty-five each month and to Amadori another ten ducats, above the twenty that he earns, to raise his salary to thirty per month."[51] Despite the differing responses to the request for leave from their duties in the Cappella, there remain several salient observations. The finest vocalists could (and were frequently) accorded extended leaves to sing elsewhere, most commonly for operatic performances, from which they undoubtedly earned considerable compensation. From the perspective of the court, these absences were acceptable as long as artists returned for the high holy days, above all Holy Week, the latter the most frequent stipulation. This recurrent condition underlines that the role of the vocal corps had gradually changed to be more ceremonial, namely for religious days of significance. In addition, the Cappella did not lack (by virtue of the documentary evidence consulted) a willing corpus of young vocalists, who could and did serve as unpaid supernumeraries. Nevertheless, the vocalists retained an esteemed status within the ensemble by virtue of their mere compensation. Specifically, Caffarelli earned the equivalent of the salary of the *primo maestro* Giuseppe di Majo, while Amadori exceeded the monthly compensation of the *vice-maestro* Giuseppe Marchitti.[52]

As the decade of the 1750s unfolded and induced an evident narrowing of focus for the vocal *virtuosi* of the Cappella, a recalibration is also evident in regard to the instrumentalists, especially the string core of the ensemble. The death of violinist Domenico de Matteis in 1758, longstanding ordinary member and principal in the ensemble, allowed the administration to provide improvements in compensation to others with a focus on string performers. The sources note that,

> His Majesty by Royal Decree of April 1758, has determined in light of the death of the violinist of his Royal Chapel to accord his [de Matteis's] *piazza* to the violinist Nicola Fiorenza with a raise in salary of ten *carlini* per month and to concede equally such raise to the violinists Emanuele Barbella and Gioacchino Sabatino.[53]

Regarding the *piazza* of de Matteis, archival materials dated two months later note that:

> His Majesty by Royal Decree of June 23, 1758, has determined in consequence of the *concorsi* for the *piazza* of soprano, tenor, and violin for the Royal Chapel, weighing the absence accorded to Giovanni Manzuoli [soprano] and the noted deaths of Alessandro Inguscio and Domenico de

---

[51] *Tesoreria antica*, # 38; f. 125v.
[52] *Tesoreria antica*, # 38, ff. 123r–125v (di Majo) and ff. 128r–129v (Marchitti).
[53] *Tesoreria antica*, # 76; f. 57v.

Matteis and having examined the report of the Cappellano Maggiore regarding said *concorso*, the *piazza* of violin has been awarded to Antonio Moresca, with the salary of twenty-six *carlini* per month, later to be raised to six ducats.[54]

This highly informative entry confirms that longstanding policies in the form of a public competition for the position of de Matteis remained in place. It is also evident, by virtue of the aforementioned salary adjustments for Fiorenza and Sabatino that the administration took a pro-active stance in first allocating raises to established members then seeking a permanent solution to benefit the ensemble. The allocation of Moresca's salary is also of interest; the initial salary in comparison to his colleagues remains modest at best. The clear stipulation that it will rise reiterates that a probationary period to gauge not only ability but also perhaps collegiality had been imposed. This financial condition appears to have been standard as it is mentioned in virtually every new appointment to the Cappella. An awareness regarding the importance of the instrumental resources of the Cappella continued to be recorded in archival materials. For example, the terse declaration that "Giuseppe Valerio, violoncello and Antonio Sciulz, tromba, both supernumeraries who served the Royal Chapel without compensation, until there is an available *piazza* for those instruments"[55] signals not only their current status and service, but also a recognition of their endeavors and in essence served as a placeholder for the future. Indeed, a subsequent entry notes that Valerio obtained a compensated position, earning four ducats per month.[56] In addition to Valerio's appointment, there is a noteworthy realignment of the string component of the Cappella. The source documents that,

His Majesty by means of Royal Decree of July 6th, 1764, has assigned the *piazza* of first violin of the Royal Chapel vacated due to the death of Nicola Fiorenza to Crescenzo Pepe, second violinist with an additional ten *carlini* to the salary he presently earns. To the *piazza* of second violin Saverio Carcais with an increase in his salary of eight ducats another ten *carlini*. To the *piazza* of third violin Costantino Roberto, with his stipulated salary. To that of fourth violin, Gaetano Salernitano with an increase of twenty *carlini* to bolster the eight ducats mandated by the *pianta* ... And to Gennaro Valente who will assume the final *piazza* another twenty *carlini* in addition to the thirty-seven *carlini* presently earned.[57]

Taken together, these entries reveal clear and consistent planning on the part of the Cappella. The identification and recognition of Valerio's efforts as an unpaid supernumerary had been clearly noted, which served as a signal for a future ordinary appointment, which in all likelihood occurred without a public

---

[54] *Tesoreria antica*, # 38; f. 223r.
[55] *Tesoreria antica*, # 38; f. 231r.
[56] *Tesoreria antica*, # 38; f. 241r.
[57] *Tesoreria antica*, # 38; f. 241r.

concorso further underlining a consideration of past service and seniority. Once admitted, Valerio's elevation triggered a fundamental realignment of the violinists in the ensemble, which reflected the existence of and adherence to a codified *pianta* (as noted in the document). The decade of the 1760s witnessed the ongoing (and often rapid) transformation of the ensemble, contradicting any suggestion of inactivity or neglect by the court despite the departure of Carlo di Borbone. Indeed, in the waning years of the Regency (1765–67), a changing of the guard occurred within the Cappella, marked by the departure and/or passing of long-time members and the emergence of the next generation. Of particular interest, a subtle transformation of the vocal corps unfolded with the deaths of Nicodemo Nicolai (contralto) followed by that of bass Francesco Caffarano. Although Nicolai would be replaced by the contralto Leopoldo Maccozzi, a clear emphasis on natural voices is evident with the admission to the Cappella of the basses Francesco Magri and Domenico Guglietti (for the aforementioned Caffarano) and tenors Luiggi Mattei and Felippo Cappellari. The instrumental complement of the ensemble experienced similar changes. In addition to the admission of Giuseppe Valerio to the lower strings (as noted earlier), Pietro Burlo and Giuseppe de Florio joined the ensemble as contrabassists (replacing the deceased Gioacchino Bruno), bolstering this section. In regard to the wind instruments, of particular interest is the admission of the oboist, Giuseppe LaBanchi. Sources note the larger context of his service as:

> His Majesty by Royal Decree of January 13 1767, being worthy, and heeding the good qualities of the slave Giuseppe Maria Labanchi, who after having repudiated his Muslim faith, and embraced Catholicism, which he has faithfully maintained through signs of constant moderation, [the King] provides the grace of freedom, having deigned at the same time, that he [LaBanchi] be admitted in the capacity of Oboist supernumerary to serve the Royal Chapel with the compensation of eight ducats per month.[58]

This extraordinary entry continues,

> His Majesty by means of another Royal Decree of January 13 1767, in addition to the grace of freedom, and the compensation of eight ducats, He has deigned to the same Christian slave Giuseppe Maria Labanchi, His Majesty has ordered that [LaBanchi] be given a single disbursement of fifty ducats, so that he can purchase the necessary materials for himself.[59]

LaBanchi's extraordinary personal narrative, journey (and undoubtedly talent) from enslavement to freedom to become a member of the elite corps and rarified social spheres of the Cappella Reale is further underlined by Ferdinando's

---

[58] *Tesoreria antica*, # 38; f. 420r. [59] *Tesoreria antica*, # 38; f. 420r.

generous disbursement of funds (fifty ducats) to obtain the necessary professional and personal articles, to ensure his success. As Ferdinando prepared to take the sole reigns of authority and readied himself for marriage to Maria Carolina, these developments would be a harbinger of considerable change within the activities of the Cappella Reale.

2 Operations, Organizational Structure, Formation, and Personnel

The reign of Ferdinando and Maria Carolina witnessed the complete transformation of the Kingdom from its longstanding political alliances to its social and cultural infrastructure, especially the cultivation and patronage of music.[60] The often-quoted representations of the monarchs as either inept or entirely too corrupt to govern the vast resources and complex dynamics (social, political, economic) of the kingdom has been well documented in past (and present) scholarship. No less than the historian Benedetto Croce proclaimed about Maria Carolina, "How one can justify a woman who, beyond the improprieties and turpitude of her private life, was caught in a series of flagrant lies and the violation of sacred vows undertaken ... I cannot understand."[61] This wide-ranging condemnation spans her personal flaws in character to a series of political miscalculations that ultimately endangered the existence of the kingdom.[62] Nevertheless, the same larger contexts, especially those engaging intellectual and creative capital (whether individuals or institutions) contributed to the unprecedented progress of the kingdom in the second half of the century that impacted virtually every facet and discipline of contemporary life. Maria Carolina in particular forged a formidable presence, influencing artistic traditions and demonstrating astute cultural sensibilities as an engaged patron of art, music, theater, and dance.[63] From

---

[60] Michelangelo Schipa, *Nel regno di Ferdinando IV di Borbone* (Florence: Vallecchi editore, 1938); Giuseppe Nuzzo, *La monarchia delle Due Sicilie tra Ancien Régime e rivoluzione* (Naples: A. Berisio, 1962); see also Cinzia Recca, ed., *The Diary of Queen Maria Carolina of Naples, 1781–1785: New Evidence of Queenship at Court* (Basingstoke: Palgrave Macmillan, 2017); Cinzia Recca, "Maria Carolina and Marie Antoinette: Sisters and Queens in the Mirror of Jacobin Public Opinion," *Royal Studies Journal* 1 (2014): 17–36; Cinzia Recca, "Queenship and Family Dynamics through the Correspondence of Queen Maria Carolina of Naples," in Elena Woodacre, ed., *Mediterranean Queenship: Negotiating the Role of the Queen in the Medieval and Early Modern Eras* (New York: Palgrave Macmillan, 2013), 265–286.

[61] Quoted in "Un'austriaca alla Corte napoletana: Maria Carolina d'Asburgo-Lorena," in Mirella Mafrici, ed., *All'ombra della corte. Donne e potere nella Napoli borbonica (1734–1860)* (Naples: Friderciana Editrice Universitaria, 2010), 51.

[62] See Carlo Francovich, "*Storia della massoneria in Italia.*" *Dalle origini alla Rivoluzione francese* (Florence: La nuova Italia, 1974); Giuseppe Giarrizzo, *Massoneria e illuminismo nell'Europa del Settecento* (Venice: Marsilio, 1994).

[63] See Giulio Sodano and Giulio Brevetti, eds., *Io, la regina. Maria Carolina d'Asburgo-Lorena tra politica, fede, arte e cultura*, Quaderni 33 (Palermo: Mediterranea – ricerche storiche 2016).

the onset of her arrival in Naples, she established a direct and deeply intertwined rapport with musical activities at court, especially the Cappella Reale and specific musicians of the ensemble. It is evident from surviving sources that select members and the ensemble itself participated in the varied *feste, conversazioni*, or *accademie* within the ceremonial life of the court on a much broader level than during the rule of Carlo di Borbone. The aforementioned occasions were often referenced in contemporary *giornali* as *gran gala* (both public and private) and bridged the performance of vocal and instrumental genres as well as dance (including the expected and customary patronage of theatrical genres).[64] Indeed one chronicler of court life noted, "Her Royal Majesty sang last night and the king sang likewise in these most intimate little academies, which they enjoy holding."[65] These events served not only as opportunities for Maria Carolina to confirm, then assert her identity, authority, and political agency, but also as purely artistic, often specifically musical exhibitions. Members of the Cappella Reale (see Table 5) were increasingly called upon to access the personal, rarified areas within the royal residences whether Naples, Caserta, Capodimonte, Portici, or Carditello. An intimate commitment to music and an evident larger, official patronage emerged almost immediately after her marriage to Ferdinando and arrival in Naples in 1768. Three months after her ascension to the throne, Maria Carolina engineered the appointment of her private teacher Pasquale Cafaro as *primo maestro di cappella sopranumerario*, unequivocally establishing her presence and voice in the affairs of the ensemble for the present and future.

Table 5 Cappella Reale di Napoli, 1768–1800

Name	Role	Years of service
Giuseppe di Majo	Primo Maestro di Cappella	1768–71 †
Pasquale Cafaro	Primo Maestro di Cappella	1768–87 †
Vincenzo Orgitano	Primo Maestro di Cappella	1787–1800
D. Giuseppe Marchitti	Vice–maestro di Cappella	1768–79f
Niccolo Piccinni	Maestro di Cappella	1771–85
Francesco Roncaglia	Soprano	1800
Antonio Piccigallo	Soprano	1769–1800
Gaetano Majorano (Caffarelli)	Soprano	1768–83 †

---

[64] See the contemporary periodicals the *Diario Ordinario, Diario Estero, Notizie del Mondo*, and *Gazzetta Universale*.

[65] Anna Maria Rao, "Corte e Paese: il Regno di Napoli dal 1734 al 1806," in Mirella Mafrici, ed., *All'ombra della corte*, 24.

Table 5 (cont.)

Name	Role	Years of service
Salvatore Consorti	Soprano	1768–87; 1800
Giuseppe Aprile	Soprano	1769–1800
Giuseppe Fabrizio	Soprano	1769–72
Giuseppe Passari	Soprano	1769–73
Francesco Agresta	Soprano	1771–93
Generoso DeAngelis	Soprano	1781–1800
Giuseppe Millico	Soprano	1788–99
Pietro Caldara	Soprano	1792–1800
Antonio Antico	Soprano	1799–1800
Francesco Bilancione	Treble	1768–75
Biaggio Bisucci	Treble	1768–69
Giuseppe Guerra	Treble	1768–69
Nicola Castelnuovo	Contralto	1800
Leopoldo Maccozzi	Contralto	1768–92
Antonio Catena	Contralto	1768–69
Giovanni Tedeschi Amadori	Contralto	1768–72
Santi Barbieri	Contralto	1768–81
Piero Santi	Contralto	1768–88; 1800
Innocenzo Lucci	Contralto	1781–93
Domenico Costa	Contralto	1792–1800
Nicola Lancelotti	Contralto	1792–99
Francesco Martucci	Contralto	1793–1800
Pasquale Masiello	Contralto	1793–1800
Gennaro de Magistris	Tenor	1769
Francesco Tolve	Tenor	1768–79
Felippo Cappellaro	Tenor	1768–70
Luiggi Mattei	Tenor	1769–79
Letterio Ferrari	Tenor	1768–95
Nicola Grimaldi	Tenor	1771–1800
Francesco Ferrari	Tenor	1780–95
Giuseppe Ducci	Tenor	1784–1800
Giuseppe Valerio	Tenor	1791–1800
Vincenzo Correggio	Tenor	1796–1800
Antonio Calogero	Bass	1768–77
Domenico Guglietti	Bass	1768–1800
Giovanni Battista Palomba	Bass	1768–72

Table 5 (cont.)

Name	Role	Years of service
D. Michele Forni	Bass	1768–85
Francesco Magri	Bass	1769–1800
D. Gennaro Guarino	Bass	1774–93
Giuseppe Saracino	Bass	1785–1800
D. Luigi Berenga	Bass	1793–1800
Carlo Moresca	Violin	1800
Costantino Roberto	Violin	1768–73
Antonio Moresca	Violin	1768–1800
Francesco Lecce	Violin	1768–1800
Francesco Piscina	Violin	1768–71
Saverio Carcais	Violin	1768–71
Giacomo Vittozzi	Violin/Cello	1768–76
Crescenzo Pepe	Violin	1768–77
Emanuelle Barbella	Violin	1768–77
Nicola Fabio	Violin	1768–77
Gennaro Valente	Violin	1768–87
Pietro Antonacci	Violin	1768–88
Gaetano Salernitano	Violin	1768–89
Gioacchino Sabatino	Violin	1768–99
Aniello Santangelo	Violin	1769–71
Giovanni Battista Bergantino	Violin	1769–81
Giuseppe Pagliarulo	Violin	1771–79
Giovanni Raimondi	Violin	1772–1800
Antonio Montoro	Violin	1773–1800
Gaetano Franchi	Violin	1777–1800
Vincenzo Compagnone	Violin	1777–1800
Carlo Camerino	Violin	1779–88
Filippo Pepe	Violin	1781–1800
Michele Nasci	Violin	1787–95
Giovanni Remer	Violin	1788–96
Francesco Ansaldi	Violin	1788–1800
Gaetano Corvo	Violin	1789–1800
Gennaro Origo	Violin	1788–1800
Giuseppe Spano	Violin	1788–1800
Saverio Chiapparelli	Violin	1790–1800
Lorenzo Moser	Violin	1795–1800
Giuseppe Valerio	Cello	1768–78
Nicola Santacroce	Cello	1776–92

Table 5 (cont.)

Name	Role	Years of service
Domenico Francescone	Cello	1779–1800
Antonio Guida	Cello	1792–1800
Giuseppe de Florio	Contrabass	1768–72
Andrea de Florio	Contrabass	1768–74
Pietro Burlo	Contrabass	1768–93
Pasquale Pumpo	Contrabass	1774–1800
Francesco Piccinni	Contrabass	1774–78
Felice Leonardi	Contrabass	1792–1800
Giuseppe Maria LaBanchi	Oboe	1768–1800
Francesco de Donato	Oboe	1768–91
Geronimo de Donato	Oboe	1768–91
Francesco Gottlieb Reispacher	Oboe	1769–84
Giuseppe Prota	Oboe	1778–1800
Giovanni Zito	Oboe	1784–1800
Giuseppe Bossi	Oboe	1791–1800
Ferdinando Lizio	Bassoon	1768–78
Francesco Ricupero	Bassoon	1774–1800
Vincenzo Conti	Bassoon	1792–1800
Baldassare La Barbiera	Tromba	1768–1800
Gennaro Piano	Tromba	1768–82
Pasquale Giuliano	Tromba	1772–1800
D. Onofrio Lorello	Tromba	1773–95
Costantino Cardillo	Tromba	1781–97
Francesco Antonio Curci	Tromba	1795–1800
Gaetano Galli	Tromba	1796–1800
Giuseppe Ercolano	Tromba	1798–1800
Vito Ugolino	Lute	1768–91
Giovanni Ugolino	Lute	1792–1800
Raffaele Consalvo	Organist	1800
Francesco Corbisiero	Organist	1768–1800
Domenico Merola	First Organist	1768–70
GianFrancesco di Majo	Organist	1769–70

Table 5 (cont.)

Name	Role	Years of service
Paolo Orgitano	Organist	1777–96
Giuseppe DeMagistris	Organist	1780–85
Antonio Colli	Organist	1797–1800
Domenico Antonio Russo	Organaro	1785–96
Francesco Saverio Rossi	Organaro	1790–96
Antonio Cimino	Organaro	1797–1800

Note: The dagger symbols in the table indicate the year of the member's death.

A new primo maestro

The selection of Cafaro is meticulously documented in surviving materials noting, "His Majesty by means of the Royal Order of August 25, 1768 has appointed Pasquale Cafaro as Maestro di Cappella supernumerary of this Royal Chapel, with compensation of twenty ducats per month."[66] His evident and rising favor with Maria Carolina is referenced not only by the allocation of a generous salary despite supernumerary status, equal to that of the ordinary *vice-maestro* Marchitti, but also in detailed correlative sources emerging from the *Ministero degli affari ecclesiatici* in January 1772.[67] Issued by the Secretary of State Bernardo Tanucci, the long missive notes:

> Since 1768, Pasquale Cafaro has been honored by the King with the *piazza* of Maestro di Musica supernumerary of the Royal Chapel with the monthly income of twenty ducats, and with the obligation to set aside his responsibility as personal *maestro di cappella* for Her Majesty the Queen. Having passed away at the end of the past year, Giuseppe di Majo, Primo Maestro of the Royal Chapel, who enjoyed the salary of thirty ducats per month, as well as another five, for monthly expenses of paper, the preparation of the bellows and other needs, the King declares as *Primo Maestro* of Music Pasquale Cafaro in place of the previous responsibility, and allocates the salary of di Majo as follows.[68]

This transparent mandate appointing Cafaro as *primo maestro* of the ensemble also underlines, albeit tacitly, that his ascension first as a supernumerary then as an ordinary holder of the most-coveted *piazza* in the Cappella Reale occurred without a public *concorso* as had often been the case for his predecessors. Nevertheless,

---

[66] *Tesoreria antica,* # 38, f. 432r.

[67] The volumes of the *Ministero degli affari ecclesiastici* emanate from the office of the Cappellano Maggiore and contain references to the activities of the Cappella Reale and at times its individual musicians.

[68] *Ministero degli affari ecclesiastici,* Registro 2, vol. 374, ff. 20v–21r.

Cafaro's career trajectory may well have eventually placed him in this role without the benefit of the queen's favor. Since 1759, he had served as the *secondo maestro* at the Turchini conservatory, establishing himself as a composer of stage drama and related genres as well as a gifted pedagogue. Tanucci's directive also underlines the longstanding mechanisms of the Cappella, that musicians often entered with supernumerary status (for the most part without compensation) and they were eventually accorded the opportunity to earn ordinary status. Regarding Cafaro's role at the Turchini conservatory, a second directive issued by Tanucci and sent to the *Cappellano Maggiore* in the same month addresses these responsibilities, noting:

> I have proposed to the King as well as Your Excellency, and the Governors of the Pietà dei Turchini Conservatory regarding the aspiration of Pasquale Cafaro, *maestro di musica* of this conservatory; who by virtue of his responsibilities for Her Majesty the Queen remains unavailable, desires to continue in the aforementioned position, providing a substitute to teach music [in his place] at stated Conservatory. And His Majesty in agreement with Your Excellency, and of the noted Governors, has directed me to write to them again, in order to make known in the Royal Name regarding Cafaro, that in virtue of the fact that he continues to serve Her Majesty the Queen, he should propose the names of *maestri di cappella* to the administration [of the conservatory] such that it can choose one who can serve as Cafaro's substitute.[69]

The unequivocal support provided by the Crown placed Cafaro in an enviable position of favor and even of authority within Neapolitan artistic circles given his status as *primo maestro* of the Cappella Reale, personal *maestro* of the Queen (which evidently seems to have continued despite the first missive from Tanucci), and *secondo maestro* (with leave, albeit ostensibly choosing his substitute) at the Turchini conservatory. Indeed, Cafaro's enduring service to the Queen is confirmed the following month, as Tanucci writes, once again to the *Cappellano Maggiore*:

> The King has resolved, that to Cafaro, in addition to the compensation that had been assigned to him as *Maestro di Musica* for the Cappella Reale, that the payment of twenty ducats that he obtained previously, however as Maestro di Cappella for the Queen, must be continued and shared with Your Excellency such that he can issue the orders of this Royal Decree.[70]

As had occurred in the past, the administration of the Cappella acted swiftly and often pre-emptively to raise the salaries of deserving members simultaneously to the privileges accorded to Cafaro. As early as 1771, there are indications of these intentions especially with regard to Giuseppe Marchitti. In a memorandum dated December 21, 1771, it is noted that

---

[69] *Ministero degli affari ecclesiastici*, Registro 2, vol. 374, f. 31r.
[70] *Ministero degli affari ecclesiastici*, Registro 2, vol. 374, ff. 71r–v.

there is consensus in declaring Pasquale Cafaro Primo Maestro di Cappella in the Royal Chapel and because His Majesty has taken into consideration the long service of the priest Giuseppe Marchitti, Vice-Maestro di Cappella of said Royal Chapel with a monthly salary of twenty ducats, it has been arranged that the salaries of Cafaro and Marchitti be equivalent.[71]

In the aforementioned letter of Tanucci cited previously and dated January 1772, a paragraph is once again addressed to the compensation of Marchitti, (underlining his status as the long-serving *vice-maestro* of the Cappella Reale), which reads as follows:

> To Giuseppe Marchitti, I confer an additional five ducats, such that he, who as Vice-Maestro di Musica, has served with distinction the Royal Chapel, and earned the monthly salary of twenty ducats, has been accorded such benefit due to the aforementioned service, and from here forward will earn twenty-five ducats per month.[72]

This acknowledgement of Marchitti's services is tempered by the fact that he was in reality being passed over for the role of *primo maestro* in favor of Cafaro and his salary would not in fact be equivalent to that of his younger colleague. Nevertheless, Cafaro's credentials as a composer and pedagogue were impeccable. His appointment provided continuity to the past in maintaining high standards and it also initiated a long period of stability for the Cappella Reale.

The Era of Maria Carolina and Ferdinando: 1770–79

In the midst of these larger administrative decisions concerning leadership and their implementation, the personnel of the Cappella endured a series of fluid, ongoing changes characteristic to its administrative profile in the ensuing decade. Bolstering the leadership of the ensemble was the admission of Francesco Corbisiero and Niccolò Piccinni, respectively as first and second organists of the ensemble, in February 1771. Piccinni was the much better known of the pair, whether as an alumnus of the Neapolitan conservatory system or the fact that he had already established himself as an acclaimed composer of stage drama on the continent. The official appointment reads, "Niccolò Piccinni, second organist of the Royal Chapel with eight ducats per month, in place of the deceased GianFrancesco di Majo."[73] Perhaps even more significantly, a series of deaths impacted the string contingent of the ensemble in the coming months. In particular, the passing (in rapid succession) of the violinists Francesco Piscina (September 1771), Saverio Carcais

---

[71] *Ministero degli affari ecclesiastici*, Registro 2, vol. 372, ff. 130r–v.
[72] *Ministero degli affari ecclesiastici*, vol. 374, f. 21r.
[73] See also *Tesoreria antica* # 76, fol. 128; *Tesoreria antica* # 67, f. 405v.

(November 1771), and Aniello Santangelo (December 1771) initiated the entrance of new *virtuosi* as documented in the sources. These decisions are rendered transparently in an entry from the proceedings of the *Ministero degli affari ecclesiastici* as follows:

> Having been vacated in the Royal Chapel two *piazze* [ordinary positions] for violinists due to the deaths of Saverio Carcais, and Aniello Santangelo, His Majesty has affected the following arrangements, the *piazza* vacated by the death of Carcais has been conferred on Costantino Roberto, regarding the *piazza* vacated by Roberto, [He] has resolved, that it pass to Nicola Fabio, and that the *piazza* vacated by Fabio, it is given to GiamBattista Briganti. And finally, the *piazza* vacated by Aniello Santangelo, it has been conferred upon Giovanni Raimondi, Leader of the Regimental Band.... 18 January 1772.[74]

The fact that these decisions occurred at the same moment as larger changes in leadership (whether Cafaro or the addition of Corbisiero and Piccinni) underlines the integrity and effectiveness of organizational structures and policies that had been developed and implemented since the ascension of Carlo di Borbone. Piscina, who had served the Cappella as violinist supernumerary since 1766,[75] would be replaced by his colleague Giuseppe Pagliarulo. This change is also noted in archival sources:

> Due to the death of Francesco Piscina, supernumerary violinist in the Cappella Reale, being vacated the salary of thirty *carlini* per month, that the aforementioned earned, His Majesty has deigned to appoint it to Giuseppe Pagliarulo, who will be accordingly a supernumerary professor of violin in this Royal Chapel.[76]

The decision to fill these *piazze* internally as well as reorganize the associated personnel underlines the primacy and significance of the string corps within the ensemble and its larger artistic mission. In the past (as illustrated in Section 1), solo voices or continuo musicians would not have been necessarily replaced by the same element (voice or instrument), whereas an apparent premium can be suggested that prevails in the cited documents in regard to the string corps and personnel, representing a noteworthy transformation from the past.

The period of *Carnevale* (December 26 to Shrove Tuesday) also occasioned changes in personnel within the Cappella, often of a temporary nature, for the vocal *virtuosi* as well as select *maestri di cappella*. In terms of the latter, one of the most frequent supplicants for leave remained the newly appointed Piccinni. For example, at the initiation of 1772 (not long after his appointment to the Cappella), the records of the *Cappellano Maggiore* document that "I have

---

[74] *Ministero degli affari ecclesiastici*, Registro 2; vol. 374; ff. 2r–2v.
[75] *Tesoreria antica*, # 67; ff. 365r–v.   [76] *Tesoreria antica*, # 79; f. 106.

pointed out to the Crown the consultation of Your Excellency on the appeal of Niccolò Piccinni first organist of the Royal Chapel, who requests leave for a month and a half to go to Rome to compose an opera."[77]

Further in the same volume, the response of the King (and *Cappellano Maggiore*) is dutifully noted as follows:

> Having the King by virtue of his authority accorded permission to Niccolò Piccinni first organist of the Royal Chapel for one month and a half to travel to Rome to compose an opera in the coming *Carnevale*; with the condition that he will not earn his salary until his return. His Royal Majesty has directed me to inform Your Excellency for his awareness, and in order to affect the suspension of salary in the specified period. Palazzo January 18 1772.[78]

Despite his reputation as a composer and longstanding ties to Naples (as well as rapid elevation to "first organist"), Piccinni had to forfeit his salary from the Cappella (similar to other colleagues in the ensemble) until his return the following March. The succeeding middle years of the decade reveal that the core personnel of the ensemble remained stable underlining continuity in performance and administration. Despite the seasonal absence of select voices (most often the soprano and alto soloists, especially Consorti and Santi respectively), an evident emphasis on enlisting new members of the wind and continuo sections emerged at the same time. In the successive years of 1772–73, the Cappella admitted a new pair of tromba *virtuosi*, namely Pasquale Giuliani (November 1772) and Onofrio Lorello (February 1773). Both Giuliani and Lorello were admitted with supernumerary status with both actions conveyed in almost identical language. In the case of Lorello, the documents note, "being vacated in the Royal Chapel the *piazza* of *tromba* supernumerary with the salary of fifteen *carlini* per month; His Majesty has filled it in the person of Onofrio Lorello."[79] As had also occurred in the past, members of the Cappella could and often did request salary increases at the passing, retirement, or departure of a colleague. Lorello's and Giuliani's names appear in correlative documents in the *Cappellano Maggiore* in succeeding years requesting further increases in compensation, and the sources do reveal a steady stream of raises.[80] In the year following their appointments, Giuliani and Lorello were joined by the bassoonist and composer Francesco Ricupero (September 1774) and the contrabassist Francesco Piccinni (September 1774). The appointment of Piccinni to the ensemble followed the death of Andrea de Florio and the allocation of the decedent appears to have been a benefit to all of

---

[77] *Cappellano maggiore*, Registro 2, vol. 374, ff. 6r–v.
[78] *Cappellano maggiore*, Registro 2, vol. 374, f. 23v.   [79] *Tesoreria antica*, # 76; ff. 194r–v.
[80] *Tesoreria antica*, # 76; ff. 192v–193r; ff. 463 r–v; *Tesoreria antica*, # 79; ff. 119r–v; ff. 151r–v. *Cappellano maggiore relazioni*, Pandetta 806-II, Onofrio ff. 289v; 298v; Giuliani, f. 326r.

the aforementioned musicians, regardless of whether they were string or winds. In particular, Piccinni's nomination notes,

> Being vacated the ordinary *piazza* of contrabass in the Royal Chapel due to the death of Andrea de Florio, who held it with a salary of eight ducats per month, His Majesty has deigned to confer it to Francesco Piccinni, who has until now served without compensation and will now earn half of the salary, that is four ducats per month. It is also ordered that the other four ducats be distributed in the following manner: that is Giuseppe Pagliarulo, Professor of Violin, who has served for twelve years with a monthly salary of three ducats will receive another twenty *carlini* each month, to Pasquale Giuliani professor of tromba in addition to the two *carlini* per month that he earns, another five *carlini* per month: to Onofrio Lorello, tromba di caccia, another five *carlini* per month; and to Francesco Ricupero professor of bassoon who has served for many years without compensation, ten *carlini* per month, which is provided to Your Excellency by Royal Decree so that he can affect the orders as necessary. Palazzo 23 July 1774.[81]

The details of Piccinni's elevation to ordinary status and with it the affiliated *piazza* of contrabass reveal the intricate administrative mechanisms of the ensemble. His appointment after the noted many years of unpaid service and disbursement of his predecessor de Florio's salary also benefit Pagliarulo, whose entrance had occurred three years prior. By extension both Giuliani and Lorello were accorded modest increases, while Ricupero had finally been recognized for his long, uncompensated contributions to the Cappella. The allocation of only half of de Florio's salary to Piccinni initially confirms the enduring managerial custom that newly established ordinary members of the ensemble served a type of probationary period to be followed by periodic increases to bring their compensation in line with peers. The death of the violinist Costantino Roberto in 1773, also provided the opportunity to realign the violin sections. The related materials recount:

> Being vacated the *piazza* of second violin due to the death of Costantino Roberto, it has been awarded to Gaetano Salernitano, and consequently the *piazza* that has been rendered vacant as such has been accorded to Emanuele Barbella, whose *piazza* has also been vacated. Therefore, His Majesty assigns it [Barbella's *piazza*] to Antonio Montoro with a salary of six ducats per month.[82]

Montoro's tenure in the ensemble lasted until the end of the century and proved to be among the most productive in the Cappella. As the decade of the 1770s continued to wind toward its close, beginning in 1776, the violin corps once

---

[81] *Ministero degli affari ecclesiastici*, Registro 2, # 399, f. 128r.
[82] *Tesoreria antica*, # 76; f. 196r.

again endured a series of transformations in personnel, recruiting some of the finest *virtuosi* of the eighteenth century. As had been custom, that year (1776) began with the seasonal departure of the vocal soloists for performance outside of Naples. As expected, Piccinni had been lured away and dispatches reveal a change in his status among the administration of the Cappella. In particular, one folio notes the following:

> The King has granted to Niccolò Piccinni, Maestro di Musica, permission for a leave of one year to travel to Rome, and elsewhere for professional responsibilities having also granted him the salary he earns on the condition that the fourth part of said salary must be paid entirely to Paolo Orgitano, who will fill Piccinni's responsibilities in the service of this Royal Chapel until he returns.[83]

This decision to allow the composer to retain the lion's share of his annual salary had undoubtedly been conditioned by Piccinni's rising status on the continent. In the following year, he would petition once again (successfully) for another leave to travel to Paris, and through these absences Paolo Orgitano solidified his own position within the Cappella as first organist.[84] In the coming months of 1776 and extending into 1777, however, the Cappella suffered a succession of significant losses, beginning with the passing of the string *virtuosi* Giacomo Vittozzi[85] (September 1776), Emanuele Barbella (February 1777), Crescenzo Pepe (July 1777), and Nicola Fabio (December 1777) as well as that of Antonio Calogero (bass voice; August 1777). As has already been noted, the *piazza* of Vittozzi eventually passed to Valerio, while those of Barbella, Pepe, and Fabio triggered fundamental changes among the violin stands and engendered a veritable tsunami of requests for either salary increases, advancement, or entrance into the Cappella. The documentation of these supplications was organized under a general heading, then registered with correlative indications in sources affiliated with the *Cappellano Maggiore*. The typical heading, in this case related to Crescenzo Pepe, reads as "Royal Chapel for the disbursement of the funds associated with the *piazza* of first violin vacated because of the death of Crescenzo Pepe, and the respective applicants [as follows]."[86] In the long list is included the entry "Filippo Pepe [requests] to be admitted as violinist supernumerary of the Royal Chapel."[87] In a similar manner, Pepe and his brother Carlo also requested, "the customary two months of their father's salary" as a post-mortem benefit.[88]

---

[83] *Tesoreria antica*, #79; f. 94.   [84] *Ministero degli affari ecclesiastici*, Registro 1, # 419, f. 83r.
[85] Vittozzi is consistently listed in payment registers as "suonatore di violino," however, he was also recognized as a cellist.
[86] *Cappellano maggiore relazioni*, vol. Pandetta 806-II 2, f. 114v.
[87] *Cappellano maggiore relazioni*, vol. Pandetta 806-II 2, f. 165v.
[88] *Cappellano maggiore relazioni*, vol. Pandetta 806-II 2, f. 124v.

Given the considerable interest generated in Crescenzo Pepe's *piazza*, a consolidated, yet detailed as well as comprehensive rendering of these deliberations (in the form of an extended summary) emanated from the *Cappellano Maggiore* in mid-July. Addressed to the musicians of the ensemble, it reads:

July 19, 1777

To the musicians of the Royal Chapel

His Royal Majesty

Being vacated in the Royal Chapel the *piazza* of first violin due to the death of Crescenzo Pepe, who occupied it, with a salary of ten ducats per month, the following have appealed to the Crown, requesting an increase in salary, and the passage of the aforementioned *piazza* to Antonio Moresca, Nicola Fabio, Gaetano Salernitano, and Gaetano Franco, and furthermore they have also appealed requesting entrance as supernumerary violinists in the Royal Chapel, Filippo Pepe, son of the aforementioned Crescenzo, Michele Nasci, Giuseppe Valerio, and Giuseppe Aguilar. And Your Majesty, directing me to dismiss the admitted respective appeals of all those presented by means of the royal dispatches issued on December 5th of this year, has deigned to order me to inform the Maestro di Musica of the Royal Chapel Pasquale Cafaro, with my opinion.[89]

It is apparent from the introductory preamble that the death of Pepe occasioned significant interest in the first violin stand as evidenced through the supplications of numerous long-serving musicians. This document also confirms the wealth of emerging talent, including Michele Nasci, who would eventually be accorded ordinary status. Perhaps most importantly, it is clear that Pasquale Cafaro, in view of his role as *primo maestro* and underlined through the virtue of royal intervention, has been accorded the determinant voice, befitting his status (and past precedent). The memorandum continues, stating:

> Having therefore listened to the aforementioned Maestro di Musica of the Royal Chapel, and having otherwise everything necessary regarding the supplicants, I have the honor to present before Your Majesty that according to the plan for the musicians of the Royal Chapel, the passage of the vacant *piazza* of first violin, and distribution of resources as follows:
>
> To Gaetano Salernitano, who occupies the second violin *piazza* with a monthly salary of nine ducats, and will transfer to the *piazza* of first violin, to him will also increase his salary from the vacated *piazza*, however, only ten *carlini* per month.

---

[89] *Cappellano maggiore*, vol. 763, f. 59v.

> To Nicola Fabio, who will transfer to second violin, to him will also increase his salary, which stands at eight ducats, another ten *carlini* per month.
>
> To Antonio Moresca, who will transfer to third violin, to him will also increase his salary, which stands at six ducats, another twenty *carlini* per month.
>
> And finally Gaetano Franco, supernumerary violinist, will transfer to an ordinary *piazza*, with a salary of six ducats per month from the remaining aforementioned ducats, [the aforementioned] ten from those assigned to the vacated *piazza* of first violin.[90]

With the replacement of Pepe rendered in a transparent manner as well as the cumulative organization of each *piazza*, Cafaro turned his attention to the question of the supplications for supernumerary status, which had already been narrowed to Filippo Pepe, Nasci, Valerio, and Aguilar. His memorandum continues,

> With regard to the other supplicants requesting to be admitted as supernumerary violinists in the Royal Chapel, as considered, that presently if there is need in the Royal Chapel of the aforementioned professors, thinking it appropriate that Filippo Pepe by virtue of the merit of his aforementioned father, who had admirably served for many years the Royal Chapel, therefore will be admitted as a supernumerary, and there will also be admitted as supernumerary the other applicant Michele Nasci, who is among the finest violinists of this capital, however, there are no positions available for the requests made by Giuseppe Valerio, and by Giuseppe Aguilar, since the latter is already employed in the service of the Royal Marine Volunteer Battalion and cannot serve the Royal Chapel at the same time.[91]

Cafaro's acknowledgement and moreover appreciation for the long service of Crescenzo Pepe manifested itself in deciding that Filippo, who undoubtedly possessed the requisite skills and qualifications, be admitted to the ensemble. The noteworthy praise accorded to Nasci is a harbinger for the future success of this musician, who continued to rise rapidly through the ranks of official musical circles of the capital.[92] In regard to Valerio (and as noted earlier), although his supplication is referenced in a terse manner, an appointment loomed in the immediate future. For Aguilar, a member of a family of military musicians, Cafaro deemed that he simply could not fulfill a potential role, underlining the regular activities of the Cappella.

---

[90] *Cappellano maggiore*, vol. 763, f. 59v.   [91] *Cappellano maggiore*, vol. 763, f. 60v.

[92] See Cesare Corsi, "Michele Nasci" in *Dizionario Biografico degli Italiani*, Roma, Istituto dell'Enciclopedia Italiana, volume 77 (2012); online https://www.treccani.it/enciclopedia/michele-nasci_%28Dizionario-Biografico%29/ (Accessed July 27, 2022; Salvatore Di Giacomo, *Il Conservatorio di Sant'Onofrio a Capuana e quello di Santa Maria della Pietà dei Turchini* (Naples: Sandron, 1924), 111; 132; 138; 297; 306).

Cafaro's extended reflection concludes with a succinct summary and supplication for approval by the sovereign. It reads:

> Therefore, in the case of his sovereign approval, Your Majesty deigns to command me, to affect the aforementioned distribution of funds, and the passage of the above-cited *piazze* in the manner that I have had the honor to present them and being accorded admission as supernumeraries to the Royal Chapel the violinists Filippo Pepe and Michele Nasci, [and] not having for now positions for the requests of Giuseppe Valerio, and Giuseppe Aguilar.[93]

This extended document offers an unprecedented insight into the administrative policies and practices of the Cappella at a decisive moment in its history. First and foremost, it underlines the continuing authority of the *primo maestro* in all artistic decisions regarding the ensemble. It also illustrates the careful collaboration with the Crown and office of the *Cappellano Maggiore* as well as adherence to well-established norms. This document represents in effect an affirmation of, and continued commitment to the highest standards with a decidedly human touch in regard to the supplication of Filippo Pepe. It also provides a clear framework for the future administration and direction of the Cappella. In fact, the death of Nicola Fabio in December 1777 resulted in another further recalibration and reorganization of the string core of the ensemble, once again meticulously expressed in the folios belonging to the *Cappellano Maggiore*.[94]

In the final calendar year of the first decade of Ferdinando and Maria Carolina's reign (1779), the Cappella suffered the loss of the venerable *vice-maestro* Giuseppe Marchitti (December), contrabassist Francesco Piccinni (January), the violinist Giuseppe Pagliarulo (April), and cellist Giuseppe Valerio (April), the last of whom had attained his desired entrance into this elite cadre of musicians. In their place would be admitted a trio of musicians, who became synonymous with the Cappella in the following decade: Carlo Camerino (violin), Domenico Francescone (cello), and Pasquale Pumpo (contrabass). Camerino's name surfaces first in notes following the death of Barbella (1777), specifically "it has been ordered that Carlo Camerino be admitted as violinist supernumerary without compensation."[95] In regard to Francescone, his name first appears earlier in the decade, specifically in May 1773, as "supernumerary without compensation serving as cellist."[96] In 1779, both assumed ordinary *piazze* (as also indicated by the presence of their names on the monthly rosters), referenced in the same source as "four ducats to Domenico Francescone, who passes to second ordinary cello; three ducats to

---

[93] *Cappellano maggiore*, vol. 763, f. 60v. [94] *Cappellano maggiore*, vol. 763, ff. 518v–519r.
[95] *Tesoreria antica*, # 79; f. 94v. [96] *Tesoreria antica* # 76; f. 196r.

Pasquale Pumpo ordinary contrabassist, four ducats to Carlo Camerino, who passes to ordinary violinist."[97] Pumpo had been admitted with ordinary status as second contrabassist in March 1779 to replace the deceased Francesco Piccinni.[98] In the coming years, their names frequently appear as the beneficiaries of periodic increases in compensation. These raises represented a clear affirmation and appreciation of the abilities and impact on the string contingent of the Cappella. As noted earlier, the passing of Giuseppe Marchitti occurred at the end of 1779. His death represented one of the longest standing and final links to the past history of the Cappella, especially to the rule of Carlo di Borbone. As part of the customary disbursement of his salary, it is noted, "In view of the death of Don Giuseppe Marchitti, the King has promoted to *vice-maestro* in the Royal Chapel, Francesco Corbisiero, to first organist, Paolo Orgitano and in place of the last, Giuseppe de Magistris."[99] The elevation of Corbisiero and de Magistris seems to have been a nod to the past emphasis on sacred genres. Although the former had indeed composed three comic operas, he and his colleague de Magistris maintained an almost exclusive focus on religious genres. The ensuing decade of the 1780s would prove to be an intensive phase of engagement between the monarchs and the Cappella Reale as well as increasing ties (in terms of personnel) to the royal theater.

The Golden Age: 1780–89

The (so-called) Golden Age of Naples traced its initiation to several key personal and political events, unfolding in fact several years before the initiation of the new decade. On January 4, 1775, Maria Carolina gave birth to her first male child, Carlo Tito Francesco Giuseppe di Borbone, at the Reggia di Caserta. Carlo was given the title of Duke of Calabria as the heir to the throne of his father.[100] His birth, as stipulated by their marriage accords, provided the queen with a place on the Consiglio di Stato, the king's council. Albeit presided over by Ferdinando, given its charge to oversee all affairs of the vast kingdom, Maria Carolina dominated this body and she did not hesitate to impart swiftly her political, social, artistic, and personal agendas. For Bernardo Tanucci, the presiding Secretary of State and close ally as well as channel of information to Carlo di Borbone (King of Spain), it signified a coming end to his long career. Tanucci's dismissal occurred in the following year (1776), setting the stage for Maria Carolina's central role in the kingdom. Despite her well-documented

---

[97] *Tesoreria antica*, # 79; f. 202v.   [98] *Tesoreria antica*, # 79; f. 202r.
[99] *Tesoreria antica* # 76; f. 89r.
[100] He tragically died in December 1778, a victim of smallpox and Francesco Gennaro, born in 1777, assumed the role of heir. See Nicola Spinosa, ed., *I Borbone di Napoli* (Naples: Franco di Mauro Editore, 2009).

personal and political shortcomings, Maria Carolina established a formidable presence within contemporary cultural and artistic life. She was a capable, even talented musician, who demonstrated evident and often astute cultural sensibilities regarding music, dance, art, and even literature. These abilities manifested themselves in the ceremonial life of the court, elevating instrumental music and dance soirees (both intimate ones and large-scale ones referenced as *feste di ballo*) to a significant level of cultivation and status.[101] In the last year of his tenure, Tanucci had lamented in a letter to Carlo di Borbone that, "The king did not hold the Council of War, [it was replaced] by a particular cantata, and instrumental music in the apartment of the queen."[102] And, as has been gleaned from her surviving personal diaries, Maria Carolina often remained dispassionate about her obligation to attend opera performances in the royal Teatro di San Carlo.[103] For the numerous ceremonial events sponsored by, and often held at court, the Cappella Reale served as the de facto ensemble in residence. The core ensemble had been often augmented by the large cadre of supernumerary musicians and for the more elaborate *feste di ballo* (held both in the city and the *siti reali* outside the confines of the capital), it drew upon musicians of the royal theater. In fact, the overlap in personnel between the Cappella and San Carlo only continued to increase through the decade of the 1770s and 1780s. In regard to the Cappella, the 1780s (for the most part) represented a moment of considerable stability in personnel and constitution under the continued direction of Cafaro. The respect for his artistic direction also extended to the orchestra of the royal theater San Carlo. In 1780, Cafaro had been tasked with the reorganization and codification of standards for the opera orchestra. In an extended evaluation published that year, he outlined the specific instrumentation, constitution, and associated standards designed to reinforce and raise the commitment of its members and the quality of their performance.[104]

The initial years of the new decade reflected a similar pattern of past fluctuations in personnel. At the turn of the calendar year, vocal *virtuosi* often departed the city, especially given the growing preference for *feste di ballo* during Carnevale at the royal theater and palace. Nevertheless, new members of the vocal corps continued to be recruited, especially with the death of the tenor Francesco Tolve in January 1780 and "whose piazza has passed [to] Francescantonio Ferrari" (son of the long-serving Litterio), who had been

---

[101] See Anthony R. DelDonna, *Naples, Capital of Dance: the feste di ballo tradition in the long eighteenth century* (Cambridge: Cambridge University Press, 2025).

[102] Rosa Mincuzzi, ed., *Lettere di Bernardo Tanucci a Carlo III di Borbone (1759–1776)* (Rome: Istituto per la Storia del Risorgimento Italiano, 1969), 964.

[103] DelDonna, *Instrumental Music*, 117–143.

[104] Archivio di Stato di Napoli, Fondo Casa reale antica # 1517.

appointed a supernumerary in that same month.[105] The division of Tolve's salary also notes that the majority of it had been accorded to instrumentalists of the ensembles, no less than Camerino, Francescone, and the recently arrived oboist Giuseppe Prota.[106] In the succeeding year, 1781, the vocal corps lost another venerable member, the contralto Santi Barbieri. His passing was followed by that of two other longstanding members, Gennaro Piano (tromba) and Giovanni Battista Bergantino (violin). The death of Barbieri and vacancy of his *piazza* set in motion a realignment of the voices, documented later in the year. In particular, it is noted that:

> His Majesty has determined that Francesco Paolo Agresta, who until now has served as a soprano will pass to occupy the vacant *piazza* of contralto, being that he had been admitted as such to Royal Service, and he will continue to earn the same salary of twelve ducats per month. Generoso de Angelis supernumerary will pass to the *piazza* of Agresta and for now with five ducats of the eighteen available, and that Innocenzo Lucci will be admitted as fourth contralto.[107]

This adroit arrangement allowed the aging Agresta a more comfortable and perhaps more feasible role, not to mention one more musically suited, in his continuing service in the ensemble, while adding new, younger members for the taxing roles of soprano and contralto respectively. The death of Piano is also referenced in this same document, naming his replacement as Costantino Cardillo, followed by the customary reallocations to other members of the ensemble. The death of Bergantino, who had served in the Cappella since 1769 and also as a member of the so-called *violinisti di corte* occurred in March 1781. The related sources note that, "The King has deigned to assign to Filippo Pepe professor of violin, who has served as supernumerary in the Royal Chapel of Naples the ordinary *piazza* of violin vacant in the aforementioned [ensemble due to the] death of Giovanni Battista Bergantino."[108] Perhaps the most significant loss to the Cappella in the early years of the decade occurred with the death of the famed opera soprano Gaetano Majorano, who had enjoyed unprecedented privileges in the ensemble (as noted in Section 1) as well as one of the highest salaries of the group. Majorano had actually been accorded retirement status several years earlier in 1776 and was even granted the privilege of living outside of the capital.[109] As with his colleagues, the response of the administration came quickly, noting:

---

[105] *Tesoreria antica*, # 76, f. 107r.   [106] *Tesoreria antica*, # 76, f. 107r.
[107] *Tesoreria antica*, # 76, f. 98v.   [108] *Tesoreria antica*, #79; f. 257r.
[109] As early as 1773, Burney had noted that Caffarelli's voice had weakened and become thin. See Burney, *The Present State of Music in France and Italy*, 2nd ed. (London: Becket & Company, 1773; facsimile edition New York: Broude, 1969), 361.

> His Majesty by Royal Order of February 17, 1783 ... being vacated due to the death of Gaetano Majorano alias Caffarelli the *piazza* of soprano of the extraordinary order in the Royal Chapel of this capital, the King has deigned to confer it upon D. Giuseppe Aprile with the same salary of thirty-five ducats per month as mandated in the plan, and enjoyed by the deceased Majorano.[110]

The laudatory note, underlining the long tenure, distinction, and achievements of Majorano's career and affiliation with the Cappella (especially the phrase "extraordinary order") undoubtedly cast a long shadow. For his part, Aprile had an extended affiliation with the ensemble reaching back to 1752. His initial appointment is noted as "Giuseppe Aprile Musico of the Royal Chapel of His Majesty two ducats per month of the ten ducats which were vacated by the death of Francesco Guardia."[111] The modest compensation suggests a status as supernumerary, not to mention his youth, and these disbursements continued for roughly one year. As to be expected for a rising star, the same payment register includes the following annotation:

> His Majesty with Royal Order of April 11th, 1754 has deigned to grant to the above-mentioned Giuseppe Aprile, musician of the Royal Chapel of the Palace permission to go Rome on the 25th of this month April 1754 and to remain there for approximately twenty days in order to perform a sacred oratorio and He commands that payment of [Aprile's] salary be suspended.[112]

In the middle years of the decade, the Cappella endured the retirement of the multi-instrumentalist Francesco Gottlieb Reispacher, while welcoming a rising star to its ranks, none other than Domenico Cimarosa. Reispacher had entered the plan of the Cappella in 1769 and his initial appointment underlines the versatility of his abilities, noting:

> His Majesty by means of the Royal Order of February 11, 1769 having decided to confer on Francesco Gottlieb, Band Master of the Regiment of the Royal Swiss Guard, performer on a variety of wind instruments, the supernumerary *piazza* of instrumental performer of winds in the Royal Chapel with the salary of eight ducats per month.[113]

Although his principal instrument is listed as oboe, there is evidence that Reispacher also performed on the other wind instruments as required by the music performed, namely bassoon, flute, and clarinet. This broad skill set undoubtedly led to his recruitment from the Royal Swiss Guard and translated into the generous salary for a supernumerary musician. The continued respect for his abilities and satisfaction with his service also emerges in a subsequent request of Reispacher. Sources note that "The King having deigned to grant to

---

[110] *Tesoreria antica*, #79; f. 257v.   [111] *Tesoreria antica*, # 38, f. 234r.
[112] *Tesoreria antica*, # 38, f. 234r.   [113] *Tesoreria antica*, # 76, f. 186r.

Francesco Gottlieb Reispacher, musician of the Royal Chapel permission for six-month's leave to return to his homeland with the enjoyment of his salary, which he earns as a musician of the Royal Chapel."[114] This liberal allocation and permission, as noted earlier, had been selectively granted by the Cappella, often reserved for the vocal *virtuosi* of the ensemble and namely, those with a continental reputation. Interestingly, he is also listed as timpanist and harpist for the orchestra of the San Carlo theater in these same years.[115] This same period also occasioned a more prominent role for Domenico Cimarosa, who had entered the ranks of supernumeraries earlier in 1779.[116] Specifically, the sources note that:

> His Majesty by means of the Royal Order of March 28, 1785; the salary of eight ducats vacated because of the death of D. Giuseppe de Magistris supernumerary organist of the Royal Chapel, the King having deigned to confer [these] on Domenico Cimarosa, another supernumerary organist in the same Royal Chapel.[117]

Cimarosa's professional profile with the ensemble continued to grow in the immediate future, parallel to his significant success as an operatic composer.[118] The final years of the decade (1787–89) witnessed a considerable transformation of the Cappella that involved changes in leadership and the entrance of new core members. The death of Pasquale Cafaro in late October 1787 ended one of the most significant chapters in the history of the Cappella. As early as 1782, the Crown had begun to prepare for this eventuality. In that year, a folio recounts:

> The King having considered the service, performed with assiduous, and zealous attention given to their Most Royal Highness the Princesses Lady Maria Teresa, and Lady Maria Luisa, his most dear royal daughters in the capacity of Maestro di Musica D. Vincenzo Orgitano, [the King] has decided benignly to declare him Maestro supernumerary of His Royal Chapel.[119]

The elevation of Orgitano had in reality paralleled that of his predecessor Cafaro, whose own service initiated as the personal maestro of the queen Maria Carolina. Often overlooked, nevertheless, is that another significant move in personnel for the Crown had also occurred at this moment. In correlative documents, it is noted,

---

[114] *Tesoreria antica*, # 79, f. 82r.
[115] See Anthony R. DelDonna, "Behind the Scenes." In Paologiovanni Maione, ed., *Fonti d'archivio per la storia della musica*, 427–448; DelDonna, "Production Practices at the Teatro di San Carlo, Naples, in the Late 18th Century," *Early Music* 30 (2002): 429–445.
[116] *Tesoreria antica*, # 79, f. 273r.   [117] *Tesoreria antica*, # 76; f. 133v.
[118] See Dietz, who has published the details of Cimarosa's later elevation in the Cappella.
[119] *Tesoreria antica*, # 79, f. 283r.

> The appointment of Giovanni Paisiello to the *piazza* of Maestro di Musica of the Royal Chamber in place of the deceased Pasquale Cafaro with a salary of twenty ducats per month. His Majesty by means of royal decree of October 29, 1787: Having deigned the King Our Majesty to confer upon Giovanni Paisiello the *Piazza* of Maestro of Music of the Royal Chamber and to Vincenzo Orgitano that of the Royal Chapel with the same associated salaries earned by their predecessor Pasquale Cafaro, who recently passed away.[120]

Although Paisiello had been in the service of Catherine II for the better part of the decade, he had been adroitly lobbying Ferdinando and Maria Carolina, albeit through their intermediary, the court minister Ferdinando Galiani, for a return to Naples and an associated position. Indeed, he wrote explicitly to Galiani, claiming:

> I am not seeking from our King neither the position nor the livelihood of anyone, because even if it were offered to me, I would not accept it. Instead, I thought that it would be possible for me to be able to obtain [a station], in addition to the one of Cafaro, who serves Her Majesty the Queen, or that of Orgitano, who serves the Royal Princesses, I imagined to be able to obtain the post of Composer to their Royal Highnesses, who wanting [it] I can compose for them a few vocal works or entertainments for their use.[121]

This same brief period (1787–89) also witnessed the retirement or death of several distinguished members of the vocal choirs, namely Salvatore Consorti, Giovanni Tedeschi Amadori, and Piero Santi. In the case of Consorti, the documentation provides interesting details, noting:

> In consideration of the long service performed over the course of the past twenty-two years by Salvatore Consorti, Soprano of the Royal Chapel, given his advanced age and the deterioration of his voice; His Majesty has deigned to accord to him his retirement with full compensation.[122]

Despite the rather direct and somewhat brusque summary of Consorti's abilities by this point in his career, the forced retirement had been mitigated by the generous retention of his full salary. Giovanni Tedeschi, the famed contralto who sang under the moniker of "Amadori," had already officially retired from the Cappella in 1784 and returned to his home of Ronciglione for health reasons. His stage career, moreover, had long since been succeeded by two stints as *impresario* of the Teatro di San Carlo (1764–67 and 1769–72). Amadori's death

---

[120] *Tesoreria antica*, # 76; f. 91r.
[121] Salvatore Panareo, *Paisiello in Russia: Dalle sue lettere a Galiani* (Trani: Vecchi e Co, 1910), 42.
[122] *Tesoreria antica*, # 79; f. 271r.

in 1787 led to the elevation within the Cappella of his younger colleague Giuseppe Millico as noted in sources:

> Due to the death of Giovanni Amadori, who was a soprano in the Royal Chapel, the King having deigned to confer this ordinary *piazza* with the associated salary to Giuseppe Millico who has already served as soprano supernumerary in the same Royal Chapel.[123]

Millico, who had arrived in Naples in 1780, lured by the return of and collaboration with Raniero Calzabigi, developed an intimate relationship with Ferdinando and Maria Carolina in these years. He would eventually assume a role as voice teacher and composer, creating dramatic works performed in private for the monarchs.[124] Despite the passing of Consorti and Amadori, the vocal ranks of the Cappella had been well supported, whether through the ascension of *virtuosi* such as Millico or the numerous supernumerary musicians annotated in the sources. In contrast, the violin section experienced substantial changes by virtue of the deaths of four members, one-third of the string complement: Carlo Camerino (1788), Francesco Lecce (1788), Pietro Antonacci (1789), and Gaetano Salernitano (1789). Each event caused not only a redistribution of funds, but also the reorganization of the associated *piazza*. The passing of Salernitano (who had been appointed *primo violino* in 1777) and Camerino (who had also held the aforementioned stand) in rapid succession initiated a burst of deliberation within the associated sources as well as the entrance of five new violinists: Chiapparelli, Ansaldi, Remer, Origo, and Corvo (see Table 5) into the fold of the Cappella. Chiapparelli rapidly advanced from his status as a supernumerary to assume the *piazza* of Lecce as fourth violinist.[125] Spano, who had been a supernumerary since 1779,[126] is noted as receiving the lion's share of the disbursement of funds from the *piazza* associated with Camerino. In particular, he is noted as:

> Giuseppe Spano, Ordinary Violinist in the Royal Chapel . . . by means of the following Royal Order. His Majesty by means of Royal Order of October 17, 1788 in light of the death of ordinary violinist Carlo Camerino of the Royal Chapel, being vacated the salary of six ducats per month, which he [Camerino] earned, the King desires that these funds are distributed in the following manner, that is three ducats to Giuseppe Spano who serves as ordinary violinist in this Royal Chapel.[127]

---

[123] *Tesoreria antica*, # 79; f. 312r.
[124] Anthony R. DelDonna, "Tradition, Innovation, and Experimentation: The dramatic stage and new modes of performance in late eighteenth-century Naples." *Quaderni d'Italianistica*, 36, 1 (2015): 139–172.
[125] *Tesoreria antica*, # 76; f. 435r-v. F. 435r–435v.   [126] *Tesoreria antica*, # 79; f. 211r.
[127] *Tesoreria antica*, 76; f. 455r–v.

Given the immediacy of the death of Camerino, the fact that Spano had been accorded the majority of Camerino's salary (one-half), and the repeated affirmation of Spano's status as an ordinary violinist, it seems likely that he also assumed the *piazza* of his predecessor. The entrance of Ansaldi, Remer, Origo, and Corvo as a veritable unit in 1788 reveals fascinating details about the ensemble as well as the larger musical establishment of the Crown. In regard to Ansaldi, his notice of appointment on November 16, 1788, declares:

> Wanting the King to balance the salaries of the violin section of His Royal Chamber, [regarding] Francesco Ansaldi, to that earned by his other colleagues, and deprived of the salary of six ducats per month earned as a violinist of the Royal Chapel, not allocated to him from that *piazza*, [His Majesty] has deigned to resolve, that from the Royal Treasury will be paid the aforementioned salary to Ansaldi in addition to the established endowment of the Royal Chapel, until there is a vacancy.[128]

This extraordinary entry underlines not only the value of Ansaldi to the Cappella, but also his esteemed status as a musician. It also reaffirms that the administration of the Cappella went to extraordinary lengths to recruit and to compensate appropriately its members, given the note that his appointment would exceed the approved budget of the ensemble. Corvo is added to the roster of violinists in 1789 and he is identified as "ordinary violinist" signifying a permanent position in the ensemble.[129] His modest initial salary of thirty *carlini* rises quickly to three ducats per month and taken together (language of appointment and rapid increase), Corvo had been accepted as a permanent member in the Cappella. The entrance of Remer and Origo occurred in rapid succession as documented on November 24 and December 22, 1788 respectively. The details of their individual appointments bear identical language and facts of service (such as compensation), identifying each as members of both the Royal Chapel and the Royal Chamber. Indeed, in correlative archival sources, Ansaldi, Remer, and Origo (as well as Montoro, Compagnone, Salernitano, and others) form an ensemble that seems to have traveled with the monarchs on an annual basis to the more modest, yet favored royal palace and retreat of Portici, located on the slopes of Vesuvius.[130] This small group also expanded to include the cellist Domenico Francescone and *maestro di musica* Vincenzo Orgitano (later Giovanni Paisiello) as well as select vocalists such as the soprano Giuseppe Millico and the *maestro di ballo* Francesco Montano. The surviving evidence suggests that this group, denoted by the appellation "Real Camera" constituted the so-called *violinisti di corte*, the more intimate and personal

---

[128] *Tesoreria antica*, #79; f. 351r–v. [129] *Tesoreria antica*, # 76; ff. 472r–v.
[130] *Tesoreria antica*, # 61.

"band" of the king. This group of musicians had been the topic of considerable controversy in the same decade, largely generated by the cultural mediator, amateur musician, impresario, and diplomat Norbert Hadrava.

Violinisti di corte

In the last quarter of the eighteenth century, Hadrava had served as secretary for the Austrian Ambassador to the Neapolitan kingdom, while also cultivating a highly intimate relationship with Ferdinando and Maria Carolina.[131] A cachet of nineteen letters penned by Hadrava survive from the period 1783–99, and reveal details about music-making at court, often involving the aforementioned *violinisti di corte* (his turn of phrase). In one of the most (in)famous epistles, Hadrava recounts the performance of a Haydn symphony by this group, noting that after several attempts on successive evenings, the outcome was disastrous, as "they played in an unbearable manner."[132] According to Hadrava, the king remained so displeased that he subsequently had the entire orchestra held under guard for several hours in order to cajole a more attentive rendition of the symphonies. Nevertheless, several weeks thereafter, in a concert organized and directed by the castrato Giuseppe Millico, "the court musicians were arrested as a result of their poor performance."[133] Despite such critical and even censorious comments by Hadrava, who had been (presumably) an eyewitness, further evidence seems to contradict his recollections. In fact, the *Gazzetta Universale* documented with regularity these events at Portici[134] (and other *siti reali*) providing indications that dispute Hadrava's assessments of musical performance as well as ability. A sense of the premium placed on these occasions and larger contexts in the frequent notices about Portici is also evident, as the queen, having recently given birth, "traveled to the Royal Retreat of Portici, where there was a *gran gala* and *baciamano* with the participation of the entirety of the Political Ministers, Military, Nobility, and Foreign Ministers, etc."[135] The mingling of political and social contexts, as had been long established in Neapolitan circles, would have been the opportunity for Hadrava to attend as a member of the diplomatic corps. An even more specific occasion

---

[131] See DelDonna, *Instrumental Music*, 105–116.
[132] Giulia Gialdroni, "La musica a Napoli alla fine del XVIII secolo nelle lettere di Norbert Hadrava," *Fonti musicali italiane* 1 (1996): 113.
[133] Gialdroni, 114.
[134] Lucio Tufano, "Accademie musicali a Napoli nella seconda metà del Settecento: sedi, spazii, e funzioni," in *Quaderni dell'archivio storico* (Naples: Istituto Banco di Napoli, 2005–6), 113–178; "Opera, Ball and Spoken Theatre at the Royal Palace of Caserta." In Leopold Silke and Pelker Bärbel, eds., *Fürstliches Arkadien Sommerresidenzen im 18. Jahrhundert* (Heidelberg: Heidelberg University Publishing, 2021), 129–173.
[135] *Gazzetta Universale*, Naples, May 23, 1780, 373.

occurred when "His Royal Highness, the Archduke Maximillian continued his holiday in Portici in the company of the sovereigns."[136] Assessments of these events are transparently presented in the *Gazzetta*, such as the account that:

> The other day the attendance by the nobility present in Portici was considerable within the first apartment and [the celebration] succeeded brilliantly to the extreme. The two Royal Princesses danced with much grace and their Royal Highnesses participated in varied games of chance, and the Royal Heir did so as well, present at the same table as the queen. Foreign Ministers presented new arrivals from abroad, and the celebration succeeded to universal satisfaction.[137]

The former account (one of many in the *Gazzetta*) provides more specific information about the typical celebration in Portici, namely, the exclusive nature of these events, the presence of local and foreign dignitaries, and the direct participation of the Crown and their heirs. In terms of the former, it is also noted that "every Sunday there will be [a gathering] in royal quarters, and dancing, to which events, guests will be specifically invited."[138] The regularity of these concerts and *feste di ballo* is noteworthy. A sense of how these events impacted the environs of Portici, moreover, also emerges, notably,

> Being significant the number of vacationers in the environs of Portici and S. Jorio, the majority have formed an Academy, located in the magnificent retreat of the Duke of Montecalvo prepared expressly for this purpose, to give superb social events with music, and dancing, in which attend also foreign ministers and many from abroad who also find themselves here.[139]

Given these details provided by the *Gazzetta* and further evidence found within related archival sources, the accounts of Hadrava lose their critical edge and can be transparently contested. Rather this ensemble seems to have been an elite group drawn from the Cappella and often accorded generous compensation and related privileges. As illustrated in Table 6 and based on archival sources spanning the decade, the ensemble included the aforementioned core of the leading violinists from Cappella.

Specifically, the ensemble represented a blending of long-tenured violinists such as Bergantino, Montoro, and Compagnone with recently elevated musicians such as Remer, Ansaldi, and Origo. In terms of the latter three, their inclusion in this group explains the language of their contracts with the Cappella and the appellation of Musician of the Royal Chamber. The evidence also verifies that for the entirety of

---

[136] *Gazzetta Universale*, Naples, March 31, 1783, 236.
[137] *Gazzetta Universale*, Naples, October 9, 1786, 678.
[138] *Gazzetta Universale*, Naples, October 9, 1786, 678.
[139] *Gazzetta Universale,* Naples, October 3, 1786; 656.

Table 6 Tesoreria antica Scrivania di Razione e Ruota dei Conti 61; ff. 100r–115r *Violinisti di corte*, 1780–89.

1780
    A Giovanni Battista Bergantino, violinist of the Royal Chamber of His Majesty: 15 ducati
    A Antonio Montoro, Idem: 15 ducati
    A Gaetano Franco, Idem: 15 ducati
    A Vincenzo Compagnone, Idem: 15 ducati

1781
    A Giovanni Battista Bergantino, violinist of the Royal Chamber of His Majesty (until April 5, 1781): 3.95
    A Antonio Montoro, Idem: 15 ducati
    A Gaetano Franco, Idem: 15 ducati
    A Vincenzo Compagnone, Idem: 15 ducati
    A Giovanni Remer, Idem: 15 ducati
    A Gaetano Salernitano, Idem: 15 ducati
    A D. Vincenzo Orgitano, Maestro di Cappella S. S. A. A. Reali: 36 ducati

1782
    A Antonio Montoro, violino: 15 ducati
    A Vincenzo Compagnone, violino: 15 ducati
    A Giovanni Remer, violino: 15 ducati
    A D. Vincenzo Orgitano, Maestro di Cappella S. S. A. A. Reali: 36 ducati
    A Gaetano Salernitano, violino: 15 ducati

1783
    A Antonio Montoro, violino: 15 ducati
    A Vincenzo Compagnone, violino: 15 ducati
    A Giovanni Remer, violino: 15 ducati
    A D. Vincenzo Orgitano, Maestro di Cappella S. S. A. A. Reali: 36 ducati
    A Gaetano Salernitano, violino: 15 ducati

1784
    A Antonio Montoro, violino: 15 ducati
    A Vincenzo Compagnone, violino: 15 ducati
    A Giovanni Remer, violino: 15 ducati
    A D. Vincenzo Orgitano, Maestro di Cappella S. S. A. A. Reali: 36 ducati
    A Gaetano Salernitano, violino: 15 ducati

1785
    A Antonio Montoro, violino: 15 ducati
    A Vincenzo Compagnone, violino: 15 ducati
    A Giovanni Remer, violino: 15 ducati
    A D. Vincenzo Orgitano, Maestro di Cappella S. S. A. A. Reali: 36 ducati
    A Gaetano Salernitano, violino: 15 ducati

Table 6 (cont.)

1786
 A Antonio Montoro, violino: 15 ducati
 A Vincenzo Compagnone, violino: 15 ducati
 A Giovanni Remer, violino: 15 ducati
 A D. Vincenzo Orgitano, Maestro di Cappella S. S. A. A. Reali: 36 ducati
 A Gaetano Salernitano, violino: 15 ducati

1787
 A Antonio Montoro, violino: 15 ducati
 A Vincenzo Compagnone, violino: 15 ducati
 A Giovanni Remer, violino: 15 ducati
 A Francesco Ansaldi, violino: 15 ducati
 A D. Vincenzo Orgitano, Maestro di Cappella S. S. A. A. Reali: 36 ducati
 A Gaetano Salernitano, violino: 15 ducati
 A Francesco Montano, maestro di ballo: 36 ducati
 A Giuseppe Millico, [soprano]: 36 ducati supplemented by 18 ducati for eighteen months rent for lodging
 A Gennaro Origo, violin: 15 ducati

1788
 A Antonio Montoro, violino: 15 ducati
 A Vincenzo Compagnone, violino: 15 ducati
 A Giovanni Remer, violino: 15 ducati
 A D. Vincenzo Orgitano, Maestro di Cappella S. S. A. A. Reali: 36 ducati
 A Gaetano Salernitano, violino: 15 ducati
 A Giuseppe Millico, soprano: 36 ducati
 A Francesco Montano, maestro di ballo: 36 ducati
 A Gennaro Origo, violin: 15 ducati
 A Francesco Ansaldi, violino: 15 ducati

1789
 A Giovanni Paisiello, Maestro di Cappella di Camera for His Majesty: 36 ducati.
 A Antonio Montoro, violino: 15 ducati
 A Vincenzo Compagnone, violino: 15 ducati
 A Giovanni Remer, violino: 15 ducati
 A Francesco Ansaldi, violino: 15 ducati
 A D. Vincenzo Orgitano, Maestro di Cappella S. S. A. A. Reali: 36 ducati
 A Gaetano Salernitano, violin (only for the spring months): 7.50 ducats
 A D. Giuseppe Millico, soprano: 36 ducati
 A D. Giacomo Lascini, [violin?]: (only for the spring months): 7.50 ducats
 A D. Francesco Montaro, *maestro di ballo:* 36 ducati
 A Gennaro Origo, violin: 15 ducati

the 1780s and even well into the succeeding decade, this group traveled to Portici at the request of the Crown. Archival sources document, moreover, that each member had been accorded a lump sum of funding to rent a house in Portici (generally during or immediately following the time of Carnevale) and they were expected to perform at the request of the monarchs. The presence of Vincenzo Orgitano and Giuseppe Millico (as well as accounts in the *Gazzetta Universale* and *Notizie del Mondo*) suggest that these musicians offered a range of repertoire and concerts spanning instrumental and vocal genres as well as the inclusion of social dance, the last among the most favored pastimes of the monarchs. As the decade ended, a further premium had been established by the participation of Giovanni Paisiello, whose return to Naples from Russia and elevation within royal music circles has been well documented. It is also important to underline the clear overlap in personnel with the Cappella. All of the musicians noted in Table 6 had been at one time or another ordinary members of the Royal Chapel. In the cases of Remer, Origo, and Ansaldi, their clear favor with the monarchs and participation in the events at Portici (and elsewhere) may have helped them to secure appointments with the royal ensemble. The cumulative impact of this evidence regarding the *violinisti di corte*, moreover, belies any assertion of incompetence, further compromising Hadrava's claims. At the least, this group may have not played Haydn's symphonies to the satisfaction of Hadrava, an ardent nationalist, friend, and compatriot to the aforementioned composer. Quite to the contrary, however, this group represented the elite of the official Neapolitan musical corps and, based on the documentary evidence, found considerable favor with the royal monarchs, court, and foreign as well as local nobility.

A Rising Revolution: 1790–99

In the last decade of the eighteenth century, Neapolitan cultural and artistic life continued to endure significant changes, attributable to both social reform and, ultimately, political rebellion. Elite associations (primarily *accademie* or similar private societies) often promoted by the Crown, generated broad contexts for dialogue and debate. A prevalent theme within elite intellectual circles of the capital focused on the past and present responsibilities of the nobility within Neapolitan society.[140] Francesco Mario Pagano (1748–99), among local academics who may be described as formed in the image of past *philosophes*, applied the social contract to existing conditions. Pagano (along with Genovesi, Filangieri, and others) addressed either directly or peripherally the entrenched system of feudalism in the kingdom.[141] The outbreak of revolution in France

---
[140] See Montroni, "The Court: Power and Social Life," in *Naples in the Eighteenth Century*, 22–43.
[141] See Imbruglia, "Enlightenment in Eighteenth-Century Naples," in *Naples in the Eighteenth Century*, 70–94.

became closely observed by local intellectuals, and for its part the Crown utilized its vast resources to monitor every development. This keen interest reflected not only the fact that Marie Antoinette was the sister of Maria Carolina, but also how the rising tide of unrest affected the European balance of power. Nevertheless, within three years Neapolitan intellectuals (often in the guise of the aforementioned private societies) corresponded with French patriotic societies. These endeavors often joined forces with the proliferating Masonic lodges in the capital, which had ironically thrived after the arrival of Maria Carolina. An ardent supporter, Maria Carolina had been opposed in harsh language by her adversary the Prime Minister, Bernardo Tanucci; the latter had even requested the intervention of Carlo di Borbone. Despite the initial opposition, the Masonic lodges eventually took the form of conduits for the creation of secret 'Jacobin' societies.[142] It had been under the guise of a Masonic lodge that the 'prelude to the revolution' took place and the first Neapolitan Jacobins were exposed, then swiftly persecuted.[143] These organizations had been deemed dangerous, given their mission to disseminate propaganda from France as well as to promote the ideals of *liberté, fraternité*, and *égalité*. The transparent objective of the Masonic lodges and Jacobin societies united in attempting to sway the opinions of the general public, while also preparing for the arrival of Napoleon's armies, should the Neapolitan Kingdom enter the fray. Against the looming tides of revolution and war, the Cappella Reale continued to thrive and fulfill its core mission to the Crown, until the eventual and outright insurrection that unfolded in 1798–99.

The initial years of the new decade witnessed for the most part the characteristic organizational norms for the ensemble regarding personnel. Among the interesting supplications found within the proceedings of the *Ministero degli affari ecclesiastici*, there is a reference to an ongoing personal issue encountered by one of the longest serving members of the Cappella. This document reads:

> Empathizing with the outcomes of the present circumstances of Antonio Montoro, first violinist of the [Royal] Chamber who with the weight of a large family and with a wife about to give birth not having means to be prepared, and given the evident needs of the aforementioned family, as well as the pregnancy of his wife and wanting to ease the same, [the King] has resolved, and commands [Montoro] to entrust himself with greatest efficacy to the Delegation of Banks in this capital as they will rescue him from his

---

[142] Carlo di Borbone had been hostile to the Freemasons, issuing an edict against their organizations in 1751. See Montroni, "The Court: Power and Social Life," 38–39.

[143] For the Parthenopean Revolution, see Mario Battaglini, *La Repubblica napoletana: origini, nascita, struttura* (Rome: Bonacci, 1992), 11–17.

significant misfortunes, in the royal name I mandate to His Excellency as well as the Governors of the Banco de' Poveri for fulfillment in the matter that regards the aforementioned bank. Royal Palace, March 13, 1790.[144]

As noted in this document, Montoro served both the Cappella and the *violinisti di corte* as well as royal theater San Carlo. The evident interest of the Crown confirms a transparent esteem for Montoro and his long service, not to mention a sense of compassion. Subsequent documents also reveal that a portion of his salary from the Cappella was set aside each month to resolve ongoing debts and continued until the end of the century. In the very same month of March, the Cappella bade farewell to another long-serving member, the tenor Litterio Ferrari, who retained his full salary, while "the ownership of the aforementioned *piazza* without pay is accorded to Giuseppe Valerio, tenor supernumerary of the same Royal Chapel, and it has been decided at the same time to admit to it [the Cappella] as supernumerary tenors Luigi de' Santis, and Vincenzo Correggio and as bass supernumerary Luigi Tasca."[145] The decision to withhold compensation from Valerio remains curious in light of his status as a proven asset and moreover, to also appoint additional supernumeraries of the same voice type to the Cappella. The administration may have had concerns about potential future absences of Valerio, which indeed turned out to be true, to pursue more lucrative theatrical performances elsewhere. In the following year (1791), records reveal that the Cappella continued to expand its large pool of supernumerary musicians, who undoubtedly sought a future ordinary position. Another group is documented on July 29, 1791:

> The King having resolved to admit to the ensemble of the Royal Chapel as supernumeraries without pay the contrabassists Gabriele Santucci, Pietro Mira, and Giuseppe Piccinni, the tenor Antonio Mombelli with the promise of one of the distinguished *piazze* occupied by Giuseppe Aprile, and Giuseppe Millico. As supernumerary violinist Gennaro Lecce, son of Francesco, and as supernumerary organist Raffaele Orgitano, son of the current Maestro di Cappella.[146]

The admission of three contrabassists underlines the significant role of this section in anchoring the string complement and perhaps the inevitable changing of the guard given the long terms of Burlo and Pumpo. Perhaps even more intriguing is the promise of a *piazza* to the tenor Mombelli and the specification of those held by either Aprile or Millico, both *virtuosi castrati*. This bold promise undoubtedly and tacitly points out the waning interest and need for the male soprano voice at the end of

---

[144] *Ministero degli affari ecclesiastici*, Registro 2; #499, f. 168v.
[145] *Tesoreria antica*, # 76; ff. 478r–478v.   [146] *Tesoreria antica*, # 79; f. 273r.

the century. Finally, the entrance of Lecce and Orgitano note their specific familial connections to current members of the Cappella as well as evidence of a continuing policy of nepotism. A particularly active moment in the fluctuation of personnel unfolded in May 1792 with the appointment of seven new ordinary members, three for the vocal choirs and four instrumentalists. Regarding the former, the death of Leopoldo Maccozzi triggered a surprising fortification of the contralto section, given the diminishing role of castrato voices in general. Specifically, sources note that "Pietro Caldara first soprano supernumerary, assumes ownership [of Maccozzi's *piazza*], according the ownership of the other contralto *piazze* to Nicola Lancelotti, and Domenico Costa."[147] In terms of the instrumentalists, Antonio Guida assumed the ordinary *piazza* of first cello vacated by the death of Nicola Santacroce[148] and Giovanni Ugolino[149] the ordinary *piazza* of lute, which had been his father's post. Leonardi and Conti had accepted the ordinary *piazze* of contrabass and bassoon, respectively; however, the sources do not indicate the respective processes involved. Past practice (and speculation) suggest that Leonardi assumed the *piazza* vacated by the death of Burlo, while Conti's appointment statement has not been located. Instead, they are both simply listed with the customary title of *proprietario* preceded by their specific instrument, beginning in 1792.

The middle years of the decade (1794–96) brought challenges to the ensemble for both personnel concerns and the deaths of core members. Giovanni Zito, who had assumed the *piazza* of Francesco Gottlieb Reispacher in 1784,[150] became the focus of an extraordinary intervention by the Crown. In particular, sources recount that:

> Giovanni Zito, oboist of the Royal Chapel, finds himself in debt to Fr. D. Luigi Mirelli, 170 ducats; to D. Pietro Ignazio, 40 ducats, to D. Luigi Figliola, 32 ducats, to D. Gaetano Chiarelli, 88 ducats, and to D. Tommaso Storace, 111 ducats, the remainder of a greater sum caused by the aforementioned items, which however by means of these Royal Orders to resolve [said debt] will be forfeited not only a third of the salary earned by Zito, as oboist in the aforementioned Royal Chapel, but also be forfeited another third of the salary he earns to the aforementioned individuals, and he will remit monthly to the *Tribunale di Guerra and Casa Reale*, and place [said funds] at the disposition of the Most Illustrious Royal Councilor D. Antonino Brancia, Commissioner, to be shared with the same creditors and until the satisfaction of the 441 ducats.[151]

---

[147] *Tesoreria antica*, #76; f. 517r. [148] *Tesoreria antica*, # 76; f. 524.
[149] *Tesoreria antica*, # 76; f. 526r. [150] *Tesoreria antica*, # 79; f. 221v.
[151] *Tesoreria antica*, # 76; f. 482r.

The significant debt accrued by Zito, the equivalent of more than eighteen-thousand USD in contemporary value, results in the extraordinary measures of garnishing two-thirds of his wages. It also suggests, moreover, that Zito's talents were highly appreciated by the administration of the Cappella and worthy of such a generous as well as compassionate solution. In the succeeding two years, the Cappella suffered the loss of two important members of the string complement: Michele Nasci (1795) and Giovanni Remer (1796) as well as Paolo Orgitano (1796), who had served in the role of organist since 1776. Nasci had joined the ranks of the Cappella in the wave of musicians appointed in 1777. Ten more years passed before his elevation to ordinary status as noted on February 12th, 1787, since due to "the death of the ordinary violinist of the Royal Chapel Gennaro Valente, the King has deigned to bestow the aforementioned *piazza* to the violinist supernumerary Michele Nasci."[152] The official notice of his passing forms a complementary bookend to the aforementioned appointment, recounting "Having passed to the next life Michele Nasci ordinary violinist of the Royal Chapel ... the King has resolved ... to promote Lorenzo Moser to said *piazza* of ordinary violin."[153] Nasci had also served for many years as first violin of the royal theater, therefore his passing undoubtedly exercised an immediate impact on these two musical institutions of the city. Similar to Nasci, Remer had served the king beyond his role in the Cappella, forming part of the aforementioned *violinisti di corte* and progressing as well to a leading role. The existing sources do not identify the successor to Remer's *piazza* in the Cappella. Nevertheless, the longstanding administrative practices of the ensemble insured that supernumerary violinists remained available to fulfill any necessary role. One noteworthy addition to the *violinisti di corte* whose tenure overlapped with that of Remer's final years was the service of Antonio Lolli. His name first appears in payment registers from 1791 and remains until 1796 as part of the select group of musicians that accompanied the king and queen to the retreat of Portici.[154] Little else is known, unfortunately, about the contributions and continued activities of Lolli. The death of Paolo Orgitano (as well as Onofrio Lorello and Francesco Ferrari) ended the storied career of this musician. In his place, sources note that "Domenico Cimarosa [will] pass to the post of first organist in the Royal Chapel ... vacated because of the death of the first organist Paolo Orgitano."[155] Cimarosa remained with the ensemble in the coming years, which coincided with the unrest of the Parthenopean Revolution and his own career downfall.[156] The

---

[152] *Tesoreria antica*, # 76; f. 224r.   [153] *Tesoreria antica*, # 79; f. 363v.
[154] *Tesoreria antica*, # 61; ff. 116r–v.   [155] *Tesoreria antica*, # 110; f. 110r.
[156] Lucio Tufano, "'La cantata di Cimarosa,' In occasione del bramato ritorno di Ferdinando IV." In Paologiovanni Maione and Marta Columbro, eds., *Domencio Cimarosa un 'napoletano' in Europa*, vol. 1 (Lucca: Libreria Musicale Italiana, 2004), 469–499.

final two years of the century proved to be the most tumultuous in the history of the Cappella Reale.

As early as 1793, compelled by the growing threats to the French monarchy, the Bourbon court had decided to join the first coalition opposing France. In November 1798, spurred on by the will of Maria Carolina, Ferdinando amassed a large army, which entered Rome to restore the Papacy as the French contingent evacuated. This success was short-lived, as the French launched a counterattack routing the Neapolitan forces, which retreated to Naples. Ferdinando and Maria Carolina along with their children and most trusted advisers fled to Palermo in late December on Admiral Nelson's ship the *Vanguard*, leaving Naples to endure a bombardment and siege, which ultimately concluded in January 1799. The surrender of the capital followed and the Parthenopean Republic was declared, whose leaders counted a notable number of officials formerly loyal to the Bourbons. Despite the ensuing chaos after the rapid fall of the city, the Teatro di San Carlo premiered a new opera by Piccinni in January, amidst the ongoing siege (and in all likelihood out of ignorance), intended "to celebrate the birthday of Ferdinand IV, our most loved sovereign."[157] On January 27, the Republicans and their local collaborators organized "the public singing of the *Te Deum* in the mother church, to the firing of canons and in the presence of General Championnet."[158] While contradictory to the Jacobin elimination of organized religion, this event represented a shrewd attempt to gain the support of the populace. The "mother church" referenced had been the Cathedral with its close ties to the patron saint of the city: San Gennaro; universal protector, martyr, and miracle-worker. Later on, in the same day of January 27th, the Teatro di San Carlo reopened and it had been renamed as the Teatro Nazionale. It featured the aforementioned *Nicaboro in Jucatan*, this time, reconceptualized "to celebrate the expulsion of the tyrant [with] an analogous hymn and ballet in the second act."[159] Although these events may appear to be peripheral to the Cappella, they undoubtedly involved the members of the ensemble given the overlap in personnel. The monthly rosters attesting to service in the Cappella cease in December 1798, coinciding with the departure of the Crown from the capital. The official end of the Parthenopean Republic occurred on June 19, 1799, formalized by a treaty validated by representatives of the French and Bourbon forces. The ensuing chaos in Naples unfolded swiftly, and the Bourbon court acted even more

---

[157] "Nicaboro in Jucatan" (Naples: Stamperia Flautina, 1799), i; Biblioteca del Conservatorio San Pietro a Majella; shelf-mark P. 106.

[158] Carlo De Nicola, *Diario napoletano 1798–1825* (Naples: Società Napoletana di Storia Patria, 1906), 36.

[159] Biblioteca Nazionale di Napoli, *Monitore Napoletano*, February 2, 1799.

rapidly to dole out retribution. Ferdinando formed the *Suprema Giunta* to act as the provisional government and reconvened the *Giunta di Stato* (or High Court of State) with the specific mission of prosecuting citizens involved in the revolution. This extended to the artistic personnel of the Crown, whether the royal theatres (San Carlo, Fiorentini, and Fondo) or the Cappella. Archival sources reveal that the royal court prosecuted artists and administrators active during the Republic, most notably the former first organist of the Cappella, Domenico Cimarosa.[160] Regarding the Cappella, as part of the vast administrative apparatus of the Crown, members would have been vetted before they could recommence royal service. Extant archival sources reveal that the Crown had reinitiated compensation to essential personnel as early as summer 1799, literally two months after the Restoration, declaring, "The King, our Sovereign, with his sacred charge, on this date of 23 August 1799, has resolved, that they continue to compensate all of the individuals of this Royal House, from subordinate leaders on down."[161] In the succeeding pages, the first direct reference to the Cappella is documented. In particular, to Antonio Guida, cellist and Procuratore of the ensemble, noting, "The King orders, from the Royal Treasury of the Kingdom, to be paid the salaries from March to the individuals of the orchestra of the Royal Chapel, a total of 433.35 ducats."[162] A series of monthly entries for the same aforementioned amount follow, confirming that the members of the ensemble had begun to draw their compensation again, at least according to this source, by March 1800. These entries continue until 1803 and also contain select annotations, providing modest increases to longstanding members of the ensemble.[163] In mid-1803, a single monthly roster of attendance lists the complete membership of the Cappella (see Table 7). The noteworthy continuity to the past is striking, verifying that the individuals of the Cappella had been successfully returned to royal service.

The ensemble remained under the leadership of Vincenzo Orgitano and Francesco Corbisiero. The string and wind complement likewise returned to their prior numbers, along with the majority of past personnel. It is curious, however, that both Salvatore Consorti and Pietro Santi, both of advanced age and long since retired, are noted on this roster of active members. This may suggest a dearth of available singers or that vocal *virtuosi* had been hesitant to travel to Naples given the larger political and social unrest as well as the prevailing climate of suspicion. Neapolitan artistic life gradually resumed in the early years of the new century and along with it, a return of the Cappella Reale.

---

[160] Archivio di Stato di Napoli, Fondo *Casa reale antica*, fascio 1269 TER.
[161] *Tesoreria antica*, # 149; f. 7r.   [162] *Tesoreria antica*, # 149; f. 44r.
[163] *Tesoreria antica*, # 149; f. 45r.

Table 7 Cappella Reale di Napoli 1800
Casa reale antica 343 II categorie diverse
Foglio #359r. Noi Fr. Agostino Gerbasio Arcivescovo di Capua e Il Cappellanno Maggiore in questo Regno certifichiamo, come l'infratti musici, così da voce, come di strumenti della Real Cappella di questo Regio Palazzo hanno con ogni puntualità servito in tutte le funzioni occorse nella medesima nel caduto mese di giugno [1800], e sono i seguenti.

Name	Role
Vincenzo Orgitano	Primo Maestro di Cappella
Francesco Corbisiero	Vice-maestro
Antonio Colli	Organist
Raffaele Consalvo	Organist
Giuseppe Aprile	Soprano
Antonio Piccigallo	Soprano
Generoso DeAngelis	Soprano
Pietro Caldara	Soprano
Antonio Antico	Soprano
Francesco Roncaglia	Soprano
Salvatore Consorti	soprano
Domenico Costa	Contralto
Francesco Martucci	Contralto
Pasquale Masiello	Contralto
Nicola Castelnuovo	Contralto
Piero Santi	Contralto
Nicola Grimaldi	Tenor
Giuseppe Ducci	Tenor
Giuseppe Valerio	Tenor
Vincenzo Correggio	Tenor
Domenico Guglietti	Bass
Francesco Magri	Bass
Giusepe Saracino	Bass
D. Luigi Berenga	Bass
Antonio Moresca	Violin
Francesco Lecce	Violin
Giovanni Raimondi	Violin
Antonio Montoro	Violin
Vincenzo Compagnone	Violin
Gaetano Franchi	Violin
Giuseppe Spano	Violin
Saverio Chiapparelli	Violin

Table 7 (cont.)

Name	Role
Francesco Ansaldi	Violin
Gennaro Origo	Violin
Filippo Pepe	Violin
Gaetano Corvo	Violin
Lorenzo Moser	Violin
Carlo Moresca	Violin
Domenico Francescone	Cello
Antonio Guida	Cello
Pasquale Pumpo	Contrabass
Felice Leonardi	Contrabass
Baldassare La Barbiera	Tromba
Pasquale Giuliano	Tromba
Francesco Antonio Curci	Tromba
Gaetano Galli	Tromba
Giuseppe Ercolano	Tromba
Giuseppe Prota	Oboe
Giuseppe Maria LaBanchi	Oboe
Giovanni Zito	Oboe
Giuseppe Bossi	Oboe
Francesco Ricupero	Bassoon
Vincenzo Conti	Bassoon
Giovanni Ugolino	Lute
Antonio Cimino	Organaro

3 *Maestri-Operisti/Maestri-Strumentisti*

In the prior sections, the sources present a considerable continuity in administrative structures and practices as well as in matters of personnel. In the second half of the eighteenth century, only three musicians held the distinction of serving in the coveted role of *primo maestro di cappella*: Giuseppe di Majo, Pasquale Cafaro, and Vincenzo Orgitano. Equally impressive is the permanence within the ranks of the ensemble itself, whether string, wind, brass, or vocal *virtuosi*. To be distinguished as a *proprietario* of a *piazza* within the Cappella represented an unqualified achievement, one marked by generous compensation and, more often than not, longevity. It is also evident that a significant number of these musicians maintained active engagements outside of the Cappella, namely in one of the local theaters, and some also served as *maestri* at the local conservatories.[164] In the first half of the eighteenth century, the *primi maestri* of the Cappella had often achieved success, distinguishing themselves as theatrical composers (above all in the realm of opera seria). These achievements had been a significant factor in their selection for leadership of the Cappella and, given their focus on stage genres, scholars have applied the descriptive appellation of *maestri-compositori*.[165] For the most part, rank-and-file members (vocal or instrumental) of the Cappella had established reputations as performing *virtuosi*. Composition remained, as such, a secondary interest in their overall activities within the broad landscape of Neapolitan artistic life. Nevertheless, a notable group of these members – the so-called *strumentisti-compositori* – from across the entire ensemble did compose and leave a patrimony of works. Although figures such as Fiorenza, Barbella, and Nasci remain the best-known of the *strumentisti-compositori* (and all three had established themselves as virtuoso violinists), other members such as Francesco Ricupero and Ferdinando Lizio (both bassoonists) as well as Giuseppe Millico and Antonio Catena (both soprano *castrati*) left a corpus of music in diverse genres that survives until the present day. Millico distinguished himself as a highly capable composer of dramatic music, much of it commissioned directly by the monarchs for private performance in the varied *siti reali*. This remaining music resides today primarily within Neapolitan establishments, although it can also be traced to other contemporary institutions on the peninsula, positing a broader circulation of this repertoire.[166] This section presents a select overview of compositions by the *maestri-compositori* and *strumentisti-compositori* of the Cappella in the second half of the eighteenth century. The genres represented include vocal music (both theatrical and sacred), instrumental works (concerto, sonata, sinfonia, and others), and music associated with social dance, the last a favorite pastime of Ferdinando and Maria Carolina. This section also considers how the monarchs also engaged directly with the Cappella in the cultivation of the aforementioned genres.

The controversy associated with the ascension of Giuseppe di Majo in 1745 marked a shift within the role of the *primo maestro*. At the time, di Majo had not produced a significant body of theatrical works on par (whether in quantity or quality) with his predecessors. Upon his appointment, di Majo favored sacred

---

[164] Salvatore Di Giacomo, *I quattro antichi conservatorii musicali di Napoli*, 2 vols. (Naples: Remo Sandron Editore, 1924); Domenico Cimarosa, Un *"napoletano" in Europa*, ed. Paologiovanni Maione and Marta Columbro, 2 vols. (Lucca: LIM, 2004).

[165] See Cesare Fertonani, "Musica strumentale a Napoli nel Settecento" In Francesco Cotticelli and Paologiovanni Maione, eds., *Storia della musica e dello spettacolo a Napoli*, 2 vols. (Naples: Turchini edizioni, 2009), 2: 925–963.

[166] There are also works in the Biblioteca del Conservatorio di Milano Fondo Noseda and Biblioteca Palatina di Parma; see *Opacsbn.it*.

compositions reflecting not only a historical function of the ensemble, but also the tastes of his patron and supporter Maria Amalia. In a similar manner, Cafaro's compositional output boasted of only seven operas and none after 1770, two years into his tenure as the *primo maestro* of the Cappella. Vincenzo Orgitano, similar to Cafaro who had served as music tutor to the royal family (Princesses Maria Teresa and Maria Luisa respectively), remained primarily a composer of instrumental, most notably keyboard, genres. Orgitano's complete works include two operas, both comedies, and overall, more sacred genres in general. For the latter two *primi maestri*, their activities reflected in large part the tastes of their patrons, Maria Carolina and Ferdinando. From a larger perspective, these musicians represented a decisive shift away from past professional criteria for selection, instead underlining the determinant role of patronage, above all, by the Crown. Of these three musicians, Cafaro – in light of his longstanding and professional relationship as teacher of the queen – has left a body of works that were in all likelihood designed for specific performance by the Cappella in the private soirées held within the *siti reali*. In select cases, it is also evident that Cafaro may have prepared music expressly for Maria Carolina as the featured performer to be accompanied by the Cappella or select members thereof (such as the *violinisti di corte*).

Music for the Queen

Cafaro's modest body of dramatic works are well represented within the historical collection of music that formed the basis for the present-day Biblioteca del Conservatorio San Pietro a Majella.[167] This is confirmed by the early nineteenth-century source, the *Indice di tutti i libri, e spartiti di Musica che conservansi nell'Archivio del R[eal] Conservatorio della Pietà de' Torchini*.[168] This volume documents the sources donated to the newly formed royal archive, which emerged at the same moment as the consolidation of the remaining music conservatories.[169] The entries, which span the dramatic stage to instrumental music, dance genres, theoretical treatises (and a myriad of subgenres), are carefully organized, specifying the items donated

---

[167] *Indice di tutti i libri, e spartiti di Musica che conservansi nell'Archivio del R[eal] Conservatorio della Pietà de' Torchini* [sic] (Naples, 1801), 4. I-Nc: shelf-mark 54648.
[168] *Indice di tutti i libri, e spartiti di Musica*, 4.
[169] See Saverio Mattei, *Per la biblioteca musica fondata nel Conservatorio della Pietà con Reale approvazione. Memoria del consigliere Saverio Mattei* (Naples, 1795). Rosa Cafiero, "Una biblioteca per la biblioteca: la collezione musicale di Giuseppe Sigismondo" in Antolini and Witzenmann, eds., *Napoli e il teatro musicale*, 299–367; Mauro Amato, "La biblioteca del conservatorio 'San Pietro a Majella' di Napoli: dal nucleo originale alle donazioni di fondi privati ottocenteschi" in Rosa Cafiero and Marina Marino, eds., *Francesco Florimo e l'Ottocento musicale*, 2 vols. (Reggio Calabria: Jason editrice, 1999), 2: 645–699.

by Maria Carolina from her personal library. Each gift by the queen has been marked with the abbreviation S. M. or *Sua Maestà*. Maria Carolina's contributions represent approximately 170 items with the majority as dramatic and sacred works.[170] Cafaro is well represented among this group and in particular, there are three individual volumes with arrangements of arias from his operas *Ipermestra, Disfatta di Dario, Creso*, and *Arianna e Teseo*.[171] In each of these volumes, there are indications of the performers, among which is frequently noted the castrato Gaetano Majorano Caffarelli, long-time soprano of the Cappella and opera *divo*. The instrumental accompaniment, as noted in the initial pages of each collection has been reduced from the original full orchestral accompaniment. Specifically, these accompaniments are uniformly Vl. I, Vl. II., Vla., Vlc., Cb., with winds (oboe, flute, or bassoon utilized at different times) and brass (trumpet or horn). In other words, the *organico* of these arrangements matches exactly that of the Cappella, strengthening the assertion of a relationship. Apart from these volumes there is also a single aria by Cafaro, whose dedication to the queen (see Figure 1) posits that the piece was intended for personal performance.[172] In particular, it is an arrangement of the aria "Dall'amore e dal timore" from *Il marchese villano*[173] by her teacher. Set for a soprano and the archetypical *mezzo-carattere* Vespina, the scoring of the aria includes violins I/II, viola, cello, contrabass, oboes I/II, and horns I/II.

Reflecting the *organico* of the Cappella, it is not far-fetched to suggest that Maria Carolina performed the aria at one of the frequent soirees mentioned in her diaries. Indeed, the queen mentioned on several occasions that she and her family liked to sing contemporary operatic selections in the privacy of their personal apartments.[174] For example, on one such occasion, she recorded in her diary (albeit in later years) that there was "music – where I sung."[175] Such events were not limited to the private, personal spheres of life, as in

---

[170] See Anna Mondolfi Bossarelli, "Gluck e i contemporanei attraverso i manoscritti donati da Maria Carolina alla città di Napoli," *Chigiana: Rassegna annuale di studi musicologi* 9–10 (1975): 585–592.

[171] *Indice di tutti i libri, e spartiti di Musica*, 4.

[172] Pasquale Cafaro, *Aria per Vespina/nel secondo atto dell'Opera intitolata/il Marchese Villano/per/S.M. La Regina/Cafaro 1776*, Biblioteca del Conservatorio San Pietro a Majella, (I-Nc: shelf-mark Rari 1.9.22).

[173] The attribution to Pietro Chiari's *Il Marchese Villano* remains puzzling as the verses set by Cafaro do not derive from that libretto. Chiari's *dramma giocoso* was the basis for later adaptations, most notably as *Il Matrimonio inaspettato*, set by Giovanni Paisiello in 1779. Maria Carolina does mention attending a performance of this opera in her diaries, yet the poetic verses utilized as the basis for Cafaro's setting remain unique to it.

[174] See Cinzia Recca, ed., *The Diary of Queen Maria Carolina of Naples, 1781–1785: New Evidence of Queenship at Court* (Basingstoke: Palgrave Macmillan, 2017).

[175] Recca, *The Diary of Queen Maria Carolina*, September 19, 1782, 131.

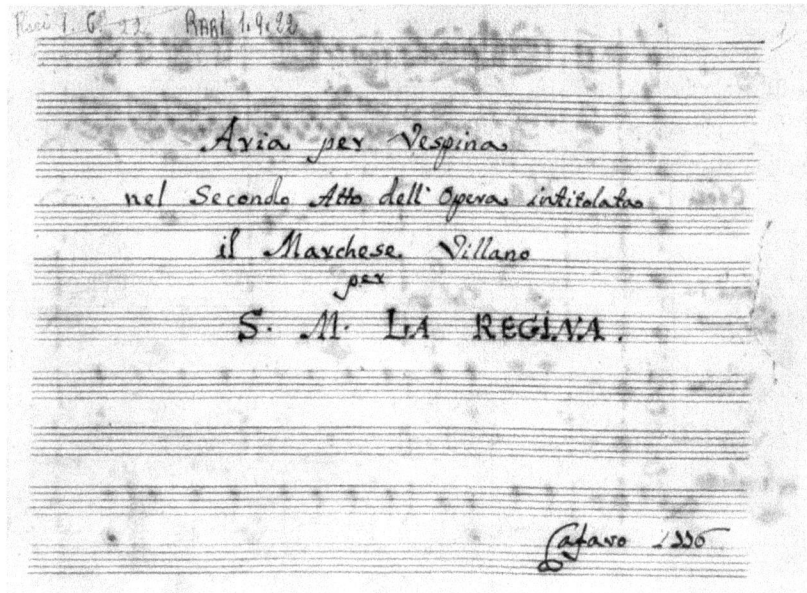

Figure 1 Cafaro, Pasquale. Title page from "Dall'amore e dal timore," *Il marchese villano*.

a subsequent entry she noted, "we went to the Academy – where we sung – danced."[176] The academy in question had been in all likelihood the Accademia dei Cavalieri, for which the sovereigns served as patrons and members of the Cappella were often engaged as part of the in-house ensemble.[177]

The introductory *ritornello* (in cut-time; G major and Larghetto tempo) of "Dall'amore e dal timore," spans a brief eight measures (see Musical Example 1). It is marked by a lilting figure in the violins, carefully underlined by regular changes in dynamic over an alternation between tonic and dominant sonorities. The declamatory vocal entry, repeats the introduction, establishing a melancholy tone for the soliloquy, namely one of longing and desire, stressed by the inflection of *appoggiature* in the violin parts. The melodic line performed by the vocalist, however, notably omits the violin embellishments, suggesting that this arrangement, while created for a skilled musician, may not have been a professional (and strengthening a potential connection to the queen). The

---

[176] Recca, *The Diary of Queen Maria Carolina*, January 2, 1784, 248–249.
[177] Lucio Tufano, "Musica, ballo e gioco a Napoli nella seconda metà del Settecento: l'Accademia dei Cavalieri e la Conversazione degli amici," in Beatrice Alfonzetti and Roberta Turchi, eds., *Spazi e tempi del gioco nel Settecento* (Rome: Edizioni di Storia e Letteratura, 2011), 378–399; Lucio Tufano, "Accademie musicali a Napoli nella seconda metà del Settecento: sedi, spazii, e funzioni," in *Quaderni dell'archivio storico* (Naples: Istituto Banco di Napoli, 2005–2006), 113–178.

succeeding change to an Allegro tempo and common time meter underscore a shift in focus placed on the vocal part. The voice part is characterized by a flowing melodic line (doubled by the violins as customary) and discloses delicate passage work, which culminates in a broad ascent to D6 to conclude the initial strophe of poetry. (See Musical Example 1.) This alternation of

Musical Example 1 Pasquale Cafaro. *Aria per Vespina/nel secondo atto dell'Opera intitolata/il Marchese Villano*/per/S.M. La Regina/Cafaro 1776. I-Nc, shelf-mark Rari 1.9.22.

Musical Example 1 (cont.)

Musical Example 1 (cont.)

declamatory and virtuosic sections prevails throughout the balance of the aria, whose cumulative structural outline presents a broad, repeated binary outline (hence, A – B – A – B). There are also ephemeral moments in which the voice is completely uncovered, rising above the instrumental accompaniment. The aria is nevertheless clearly weighted toward broader, more declamatory phrases, allowing a range of expression (and, of course, reflecting the abilities of the dedicatee). Nevertheless, the technical and expressive resources presented in this piece indicate that it was conceived for a soprano of sound musical abilities grounded in a thorough training.

The soliloquy also points to the skills of Cafaro, who although he had largely set aside the composition of stage drama, continued to be in tune with contemporary trends. The choice of an aria associated with the ascendant comic forms of contemporary Naples and evident compositional skill remain impressive. The survival of the aria as well as individual volumes of arrangements from his earlier operas and a contemporary cultivation of sacred genres, point directly toward the activities and engagement of the Cappella. This body of repertoire also posits a change in direction from organizational norms regarding the ensemble associated with Carlo di Borbone and Maria Amalia. In particular, a pivot toward a more wide-ranging utilization of the Cappella beyond his longstanding engagement with liturgical functions and sacred music.[178] In addition, each of the selections contained in the manuscript reflect operas donated by Maria Carolina to the newly established royal archive.[179] Finally, the meticulous juxtaposition of Neapolitan and Austro-German composers, above all the queen's expressed favorites Gluck and Schuster, bolster the evident connection to the Cappella as part of their musical repertory and for the personal performance of Maria Carolina. Indeed, a second manuscript held in the Conservatory Library of Naples presents a broad collection of arias from contemporary operas performed in the city. It is not limited to those by Cafaro, albeit his contributions form the greatest number, also including soliloquies by Giovanni Paisiello, Antonio Sacchini, Giacomo Insanguine, Rutini, Christoph Gluck, and Johann Schuster. All of the selections are arranged for soprano and the same instrumental accompaniment as Cafaro's "Dall'amore e dal timore," once again positing a connection and potential preparation for the Cappella.

String virtuosi: Santangelo, Montoro, Nasci and Chiapparelli

From the initiation of the early modern period, the Cappella boasted of an uninterrupted line of string *virtuosi*, especially the leading violinists of the city.[180] Among the ranks of the ensemble for more than twenty-years (1750–72), Aniello Santangelo remained a stalwart of the Cappella. Scant information

---

[178] See *Composizioni vocali profane*, (I-Nc: shelf-mark Arie 41).
[179] *Indice di tutti i libri, e spartiti di Musica*.
[180] Guido Olivieri, *String Virtuosi in Eighteenth-Century Naples: Culture, Power, and Music Institutions* (Cambridge: Cambridge University Press, 2024); Olivieri, "La musica strumentale a Napoli," in Francesco Cotticelli and Paologiovanni Maione, eds., *Storia della musica e dello spettacolo a Napoli: Il Seicento* (Naples: Turchini edizioni, 2020), 1493–1535; Olivieri, "Condizione sociale dei musicisti nella Napoli del '700," in Pierpaolo DeMartino, ed. *Napoli Musicalissima: Studi in onore del 70.mo compleanno di Renato Di Benedetto* (Lucca: LIM,

survives beyond his service in the royal chapel, however, DiGiacomo records that he also fulfilled the role of *maestro di violino* at the Turchini conservatory in the years 1759–71.[181] This station of distinction undoubtedly placed him in a position to develop a network of colleagues and younger violinists, who could join the ranks of the Cappella (or other ensembles of the city). Indeed, Santangelo would be succeeded by his younger contemporary and fellow member of the Cappella, Nicola Fabio, at the Turchini.[182] Santangelo's surviving music reflects the primary instrumental genres, including a collection of sonatas for two violins and cello; two concertos for flute and strings; and a sinfonia.[183] The manuscript for the twelve sonatas bears the indication of Op. 1, however, no date of composition is provided.[184] Specified as *trii*, the majority of these compositions are conceived in the four movement, S-F-S-F outline of the trio sonata. This relationship is strengthened, moreover, through the tonal unity of most of the pieces as well as the reliance on binary formal structures (although the reprise is often written out in full or bears some telescoping or overall reduction). The presence of dance movements (such as gigue) and associated tempo markings further underline the relationship to the trio sonata. Nevertheless, the cello part is limited to few or no figures suggesting, (but not confirming), a purely string texture. Of the twelve sonatas, only the third and eighth are conceived in a three-movement outline of F – S – F. These two compositions represent the most musically innovative and progressive of the group, pointing to the future.

Sonata III spans one-hundred ninety-one bars and presents a broad rounded-binary structure. The A section extends eighty bars and it is marked by a multitude of melodic ideas, introduced primarily by the first violin. Nevertheless, the second violin and cello engage often in the musical discourse, establishing themselves on an equal level and frequently filling out the essential texture of the trio. The opening gesture is characteristic to the movement, outlining an immediate octave plunge and return, followed by a scalar descent (see Musical Example 2; mm. 1–4) stressing scale degrees 7, 5, and 3. The immediate sequential continuation of the opening on the submediant posits a shift to g minor in mm. 3–4 (thus transposed down a third), again stressing the aforementioned scale degrees, and culminates in an abrupt leap upward to the new tonic. Played by all three instruments, there are clear suggestions of the Falling Thirds schema. This bold gesture also evokes a "Zweier" (a term

---

2006), 45–68; Olivieri, *Marchitelli, Mascitti e la musica strumentale napoletana fra Sei e Settecento* (Lucca: LIM, 2023).

[181] Di Giacomo, *I quattro antichi conservatorii musicali*, vol. I, 291.
[182] Di Giacomo, *I quattro antichi conservatorii musicali*, 291.
[183] See Aniello Santangelo, *Opacsbn.it*.
[184] Aniello Santangelo, *Trii* (I-Nc, shelf-mark 34.3.21).

Musical Example 2 Aniello Santangelo. *Sonata III* in *Trii*. I-Nc, shelf-mark 34.3.21.

utilized by Riepel and Koch), that is, an initial two-bar phrase, immediately transposed down by a third. Of interest is the open-ended melodic closure on scale degree three of the first pair, which then proceeds to a stronger more closed arrival in the second on scale degree one. Taken as a whole, the unison idea posits contrapuntal ideas that saturate the movement, whether the rapid octave descent, the broken octave figures, or ascending or descending scalar passages. The tapering gesture (mm. 3–4) elides with the consequent phrase, rising two octaves before cascading downward to affect a half-cadence.

The initial subsection (of A) takes flight through a series of successive melodic ideas, each with distinctive elements. The first unfolds in balanced, four-bar phrases, marked by the aforementioned angular unison figure as well as broken octaves and repetitive descending ideas. The second (mm. 14–21) offers a subtle stylistic counterpoint, initiating with a rhythmic triplet gesture followed by an octave leap then descent that includes a prominent flatted-sixth degree. The third (mm. 26–33) synthesizes prior ideas whether the repetitive scalar passages (ascending or descending), followed by broken triadic gestures punctuated by a cadential extension spanning an extra measure. The balance of the initial subsection of A (mm. 34–69) takes a similar approach, namely a series of melodic phrases, however, with a clear harmonic leaning toward the dominant harmony and key, underlined by a concluding half cadence (on C) in m. 80. Santangelo initiates the B section through a familiar compositional gambit, the return of the initial unison melodic figure (from the opening mm. 1–4), here stated in the prevailing F major. What follows are telescoped recalls of earlier material leading to bravura passages highlighting the technical prowess (featuring contrast in registers, diverse articulations, broken octaves, and rapid double stops) of the soloist in mm. 103–124. These ideas are rounded off by transitional passages that resemble earlier material (as opposed to a literal reprise), building tension to prepare for the return of the A section in m. 138. The ensuing reprise spans the final portion of the initial movement, referring to earlier melodic material, while reiterating primarily the return to the tonic harmony. Taken altogether, the initial movement of Sonata III offers an abundance of progressive features: the wealth of melodic ideas, idiomatic writing for all three instruments, balanced musical textures marked by motivic and rhythmic interplay, symmetrical melodic structures, as well as transparent and equally proportioned formal components. This composition also points to a body of repertoire composed by members of the Cappella that has been largely forgotten or overlooked in contemporary scholarship.

Among the longest tenured members of the Cappella, whose service overlapped with Santangelo and literally several generations of violinists, Antonio Montoro (as noted in Section 2) entered the ensemble in 1773 and performed until the beginning of the nineteenth century.[185] Indeed, the final notice within the Neapolitan archives referencing the violinist recount "Settima Bandinelli, widow of the Chamber Violinist Antonio Montoro," documenting the disbursement of his pension to her and dated September 23, 1815.[186] His professional activities within the service of the court had initiated as early as 1769, when he is recorded as a violinist in the San Carlo orchestra. He held this position concurrently with his role within the Cappella, a common occurrence in the city among professional musicians. Montoro is also frequently documented as among the musicians who received additional compensation for composing and performing the music of the *feste di ballo* celebrations held each year in the royal theater (and other locations) during Carnevale.[187] For example, Montoro was compensated a total of 16 ducats ($842.88), "eight for having performed as first violin ... and another eight for the composition of eight minuets."[188] This dual role as performer and composer resulted in the generous compensation, a figure not unusual for the elite class of musicians that served the Crown. Montoro's name appears frequently in surviving sources related to the musical life within the environs of the court. In fact, the *feste* were also often performed in private, as noted in a correlative archival source, citing Montoro as having been compensated "three ducats for his service ... in having played in the eight performances of contradances that occurred during *Carnevale* for the enjoyment of their Royal Majesties."[189] It is also evident that Montoro maintained

---

[185] See *Tesoreria antica Scrivania di Razione e Ruota dei Conti*, #76; f. 196r.

[186] Archivio di Stato di Napoli, Fondo *Casa reale antica*; fascio 2969; f. 20r.

[187] See DelDonna, *Naples, Capital of Dance: The feste di ballo tradition in the long eighteenth century* (Cambridge: Cambridge University Press, 2025).

[188] Paola De Simone, "La Cerere placata di Niccolò Jommelli," appendix #3; Entry 408, 852.

[189] Giulia Di Dato, Teresa Mautone, Maria Melchionne, and Carmela Petrarca, "Notizie dallo Spirito Santo: la vita musicale a Napoli nelle carte bancarie (1776–1785)," in Domenico Cimarosa, *Un "napoletano" in Europa*, 2, 1164.

a recognized profile as a composer; however, only a small portion of his music has survived to the present. In addition to the aforementioned dance pieces, there is the cantata *Ninna, per il Santissimo Natale*, which takes as its basis the eponymous Nativity hymn.[190] Presented within a modest volume of sacred music alongside single works by Cafaro and Hasse respectively (both devoted to the Nativity), this collection is among the manuscripts donated to the royal archive by Maria Carolina, bolstering Montoro's importance to the court as an instrumentalist and composer.[191] Spanning four movements with two vocal interludes, this setting of the Christmas hymn features two soprano soloists, SATB choir, violin I & II, viola, cello, and contrabass, clarinets, horns, and bassoon. The highly lyrical yet often declamatory recounting of the spiritual narrative distinguishes Montoro as a talented composer of vocal music. Given the provenance of this source (as among those donated to the royal archive by Maria Carolina) and a scoring easily rendered by the Cappella, this piece may have been intended for private performance for the monarchs. In addition to this cantata, Montoro is survived by a collection of seven *sinfonie*. These *sinfonie* bear the inscription "Dedicated to His Most Royal Highness, the Hereditary Prince,"[192] suggesting another intimate connection to the Crown. Although the manuscript does not bear a date, given the emphasis that the queen placed on musical performance and instruction with her children, one can suggest that this piece had been dedicated to Francesco di Borbone (1777–1830), the second male issue of Ferdinando and Maria Carolina.[193] These modest compositions, similar to the aforementioned cantata, bear a similar scoring (violin I & II, viola, cello, contrabass, pairs of oboes and horns) that point to the Cappella as well as the instrumental tradition of the *sinfonia* in Naples. Indeed, the limited history of the *sinfonia* in Naples has largely been confined to its operatic function in the eighteenth century.[194] Nevertheless, there is evidence of interest and cultivation within the inner circle of the Crown. In addition to the Montoro manuscript, a compilation of *sinfonie* exists in the Biblioteca del Conservatorio San Pietro a Majella, whose provenance points toward the Cappella. The volume contains bound orchestral parts and bears the handwritten inscription "Sinfonie di Cimarosa, Sterckel [sic], Tritta

---

[190] Antonio Montoro, *Ninna, per il Santissimo Natale*, *Composizioni vocali sacre*, Biblioteca del Conservatorio San Pietro a Majella (I-Nc: shelf-mark 21.5.18, 77–136).
[191] *Indice di tutti i libri, e spartiti*, 4
[192] Antonio Montoro, *Sette sinfonie con due violini, due oboi, corni, e basso*, Biblioteca del Conservatorio di Milano Fondo Noseda M 29–9.
[193] Francesco became the heir with the death of his brother Carlo Tito in 1778.
[194] See Mary Sue Morrow and Bathia Churgin, eds., *The Symphonic Repertoire, Vol. I: The Eighteenth-Century Symphony* (Bloomington: Indiana University Press, 2012), 1–39, 411–471; see also Marita Petzoldt McClymonds, "The Italian Opera Sinfonia 1720 to 1800," in Morrow and Churgin, eds., *The Symphonic Repertoire, Vol. I.*, 117–169.

[sic], Cimarosa, Gabellone, Naumann, Schusther [sic], e Guglielmi."[195] The contents reflect, once again, a juxtaposition of Austro-German and Neapolitan musicians, all of whom had been within the orbit of the court and reflect the tastes of Ferdinand and Maria Carolina. The uniform orchestration of these works as two violins, two violas, cello, contrabass, two oboes, two flutes, and two horns is consistent to both the instrumental core of the Cappella Reale and Montoro's sinfonia, establishing potential links to the cultivation of the genre.

Each of Montoro's seven *sinfonie* present a single movement, marked in a rapid tempo and spanning modest dimensions (anywhere from seventy-seven to one-hundred forty-nine bars in length). The harmonic compass of these works is equally unpretentious, not exceeding three accidentals. From the perspective of formal structure, Montoro opts for transparent rounded binary outlines and melodic material grounded in the schemata of the *partimento* tradition. The seventh *sinfonia* offers a typical representation of this collection. Scored for the full instrumental component noted earlier, the movement presents an E-flat major tonality and Allegro non tanto tempo in common time. The formal parameters have been rendered as a rounded binary structure distinguished by a transparent harmonic progression. The opening gesture alludes to characteristic melodic ideas of the Neapolitan sinfonia tradition and posits suggestions of diverse schemata. In particular, the first violin presents the melody, which, after the initial octave fall, (outlining a Triadic Descent) rises a fifth before returning to the tonic in a simple, lyrical gesture. The first oboe doubles this line (an octave higher), and its continuation at first proposes a Do-Re-Mi, but continues to ascend to the fifth scale degree on the downbeat of measure 10, effecting a half-cadence (or medial caesura) rather than continuing to develop into an Overture schema (see Musical Example 3; mm. 1–16).[196]

This introductory gambit is underlined by rapid changes in dynamic (from *forte* to *dolce*), octave displacement, and aggressive tremolos. The suggestion of schemata, from the initial Triadic Descent to the Do-Re-Mi, (and even a nascent Overture schema), ground this sinfonia in the Neapolitan tradition. Beginning in m. 11, a Do-Re-Mi emerges now in the dominant key of B-flat, precipitating another half cadence in mm. 15–16 with the tenor clausula in the bass. This concluding element of the opening appears as part of a trimodular block. The oboes also occupy an important role in the presentation of the thematic material. As the initial figure culminates in a half-cadence marked *forte*, the oboes enter in thirds to solidify the dominant key with a lyrical

---

[195] *Sinfonie di Cimarosa, Sterckel* [sic], *Tritta* [sic], *Cimarosa, Gabellone, Naumann, Schusther* [sic], *e Guglielmi*, Biblioteca del Conservatorio San Pietro a Majella (I-Nc: shelf-mark MS 66).
[196] See DelDonna, *Instrumental Music*, 269–270.

Musical Example 3 Antonio Montoro. *Sette sinfonie con due violini, due oboi, corni, e basso*. Biblioteca del Conservatorio di Milano Fondo Noseda M 29–9.

Musical Example 3 (cont.)

descending melody. In a similar manner to the Santangelo trio, the dominant key is ultimately affirmed by the reprise of the opening gesture in B-flat, slightly telescoped to a single phrase, then succeeded by a digression to g minor. The foray to g minor (the dominant minor) builds harmonic tension, underlined by string tremolos and changes of volume, leading to the reprise of the A section as well as its thematic material. Montoro's sinfonia is an excellent representation of the Neapolitan cultivation of this genre and the composer himself. Given the larger social contexts of a potential performance, within either the private spheres of the *siti reali,* the (physical) Cappella itself, or even an organization such as the Accademia dei Cavalieri,[197] these works are perfectly tailored to expectations. Namely they offer restraint in length, conception, and content, while also displaying an evident and expert compositional craft, indicative of both the milieu of music-making within the Cappella and the class of *maestri-strumentisti* active in this context.

In comparison to his colleagues within the Cappella, there is a remarkable amount of surviving information about the career of Michele Nasci. Trained at the Conservatorio di San Onofrio, Nasci entered this institution on June 19, 1758, according to DiGiacomo's chronicle and extant documents.[198] The latter materials, moreover, claim "he graduated as a virtuoso from the conservatory on June 19, 1766 and as a token of appreciation for his contributions was awarded his bed."[199] At the San Onofrio, Nasci had been a student of Saverio Carcais, *maestro di violino* and long-term member of the Cappella. This relationship undoubtedly helped the younger musician establish himself first as a supernumerary in the Cappella, then obtain an ordinary position. Nasci had also studied, in all likelihood, composition with either Carlo Cotumacci or Giuseppe Dol, who served as the *maestri di cappella.*[200] Charles Burney's

---

[197] Tufano, "Accademie musicali a Napoli," 113–178; Tufano, "Il mestiere del musicista: formazione, mercato, consapevolezza, immagine," in Francesco Cotticelli and Paologiovanni Maione, eds., *Storia della musica e dello spettacolo a Napoli: Il Settecento,* 2: 733–771.

[198] See Cesare Corsi, "Michele Nasci," in *Dizionario Biografico degli Italiani,* Roma, Istituto dell'Enciclopedia Italiana, volume 77 (2012); online https://www.treccani.it/enciclopedia/michele-nasci_%28Dizionario-Biografico%29/ (accessed July 27, 2022; Di Giacomo, *Il Conservatorio di Sant'Onofrio a Capuana,* 111; 132; 138; 297; 306; Ulisse Prota-Giurleo, *La grande orchestra del R. Teatro di San Carlo nel Settecento* (Naples, 1927); Guido Gasperini and Franca Gallo, *Catalogo delle opere musicali del Conservatorio di musica S. Pietro a Majella di Napoli* (Parma, Biblioteca Musica Bononiensis, 1934; reprint Arnaldo Forni editore, 1988), 427; 620; 662; Di Dato, et al. "Notizie dello Spirito Santo," 2, 699, 961, 971, 1008, 1098, 1119, 1126, 1127.

[199] Corsi cites the following document on Nasci: Napoli, Conservatorio di S. Pietro a Majella, Archivio storico, Conservatorio di S. Onofrio a Capuana, *Rollo degli alunni e dei convittori* [1752–70], c. 54r. See Corsi, "Michele Nasci" in *Dizionario Biografico degli Italiani,* Rome, Istituto dell'Enciclopedia Italiana, volume 77 (2012); online www.treccani.it/enciclopedia/michele-nasci_%28Dizionario-Biografico%29/ (accessed July 25, 2022).

[200] Di Giacomo, *Il Conservatorio di Sant'Onofrio a Capuana,* 132–137.

chronicle of his visit to Naples in 1771 has provided a wealth of information about Nasci's activities and career. In particular, Burney recounted: "Signor Nasci, who leads the band at the comic opera in the theatre *de Fiorentini*, played on the violin in the Dominican's performance, and afterward in some of his own trios, which are extremely pretty, with a very uncommon degree of grace and facility."[201]

It has also been assumed that since this performance occurred in the residence of Sir William Hamilton, Ambassador to Great Britain, it led to the publication of Nasci's early sonatas in London the same year.[202] Nevertheless, surviving archival documents in Naples dispute Burney's assertion about Nasci's employment at the Fiorentini. These sources verify that by at least 1769, Nasci had been retained within the artistic personnel of the royal court. His name appears on a list of musicians who performed for the six *feste di ballo* organized at the Reggia di Caserta during Carnevale in 1769.[203] Two years later, Nasci is cited as *primo violino* for the orchestra of the Teatro Nuovo, not the Fiorentini, who performed at Caserta for Carnevale in 1771.[204] Two years further on in 1773, Nasci is still listed as *primo violino* at the Nuovo with Carlo Camerino remaining in the position of *primo violino* for the Fiorentini ensemble.[205] In all likelihood, this arrangement held until 1778, the year in which Camerino assumed leadership of the orchestra at the Teatro di San Carlo.[206] What remains unclear is whether Nasci then took the leadership of the Fiorentini? It is known that in 1779, he is cited as *primo violino* for the ensemble at the newly opened Teatro del Fondo.[207] One could speculate that he remained in this role until he joined the San Carlo orchestra in 1788 as *primo violino*, a position he held until 1793. In the interim, Nasci also joined the ranks of the Cappella as supernumerary violinist in 1777 (see Section 2) and eventually earned a *piazza*. Nasci also remained active as a pedagogue, serving as *maestro di violino* at the Conservatorio di S. Onofrio. Although payment records survive only for the period of 1780–83, Di Giacomo lists his service over the span of 1771–95 and that he succeeded his teacher Carcais.[208] The violinist earned an annual salary of 54 ducats, a considerable sum in the eighteenth century.[209] Nasci is also listed by Di

---

[201] Burney, *The Present State of Music in France and Italy*, 357.
[202] The *Sonate sei di Cembalo con Accompagnamento di Violino* were published in 1771 by Welcker.
[203] Archivio di Stato di Napoli; fondo *Casa Reale Amministrativa* # 2222; f. 269r.
[204] Archivio di Stato di Napoli; fondo *Casa Reale Amministrativa* # 2223; f. 17.
[205] Archivio di Stato di Napoli; fondo *Archivio Farnesiano* # 1820, Vol. II; ff. 19, 23, 26.
[206] Archivio di Stato di Napoli; fondo *Archivio Farnesiano* # 1842, Vol. III; f. 15.
[207] See Corsi, "Michele Nasci" in *Dizionario Biografico degli Italiani*.
[208] DiGiacomo, *I quattro antichi conservatorii*, Vol. I, 124.
[209] See Di Dato, et al., "Notizie dello Spirito Santo," 699. See also entry #292.

Giacomo as *maestro di violino*, succeeding his colleague Camerino, at the Pietà dei Turchini conservatory.[210] There is also evidence that he substituted for Camerino as concert master of the ensemble at the Accademia dei Cavalieri for a single season.[211] This engagement with multiple ensembles (the Cappella and local theaters) and institutions (such as the conservatories and Accademia) throughout the capital city formed the characteristic narrative for Nasci and his contemporaries. It was also complemented by his activities as a composer.

Although his surviving compositions are not numerous, they do reflect the larger cultivation in Naples of instrumental chamber music (sonatas, trios, and dance pieces, the last of these genres conceived as a collection of "corrente") and orchestral genres (almost exclusively concertos). Marked *Allegro* in the meter of two-four and key of G major, the third *corrente* for violin and cello departs from the typical binary construct of most dances.[212] Instead, Nasci opts for an expansive sonata form spanning 361 bars and reflecting contemporary formal protocols. The solo part requires impeccable technical and interpretative skills, undoubtedly pointing toward the abilities of the composer himself. The lyrical opening expresses the initial thematic idea unfolding in three four-bar phrases (the typical "sentence presentation") taking the shape of an a b b outline (or antecedent – consequent – consequent). These phrases disclose a triadic ascent schema, nested with an Overture schema, eventually reaching a ninth (or A6) before cascading downward to affect a Meyer (expressed as an imperfect authentic cadence) in measure 8, followed by an immediate repetition of the consequent phrase and schema (mm. 9–12; see Musical Example 4).

The reprise of the initial figure of the antecedent phrase (in m. 13) is joined to that of the consequent then subjected to immediate embellishment, extension, and development. This establishes the focus of the entire Exposition section as a series of adaptations on the primary motivic ideas from the "a" and "b" phrases. The careful articulations (*detaché* alternating with legato) highlight a series of melodic variations that unfold across the full range of the instrument. The melodic lines alternate at times with more contrapuntal episodes engaging the accompaniment in a playful back-and-forth. In terms of the latter, the frequent presence of treble clef and an entire absence of bass figures strongly suggests the cello as the preferred accompaniment. Similar to the violin, the cello requires a noteworthy technique and exploits the outlines of the instrument's range. The utilization of a keyboard,

---

[210] DiGiacomo, *I quattro antichi conservatorii*, vol. II, 283.
[211] Di Dato, et al., "Notizie dello Spirito Santo," 699; footnote 171.
[212] Michele Nasci, Corrente III in *Dieci correnti per violino*. I-Nc, shelf-mark MS 6273; 22.6.19.

Musical Example 4 Michele Nasci, Corrente III in *Dieci correnti per violino*. I-Nc, shelf-mark MS 6273; 22.6.19.

however, cannot be definitively ruled out in the sonata. The harmonic compass of this *corrente*, like most of the others, passes through a series of closely related modulations arriving at the dominant tonality as the Exposition closes.

The Development section ensues after the customary double bar, immediately referencing the appoggiatura of the "a" motive that opens the sonata. This section opts for a more playful, engaged style between the two parts, marked by contrapuntal exchanges of a descending figure and harmonic instability, albeit a well-proportioned length to balance the Exposition. As this section winds toward a close, the dominant tonality (D major) emerges again to prepare for the Recapitulation. The concluding section matches in content and length that of the Exposition. There is also an evident expansion to highlight the drama of the conclusion. The third *corrente* is an excellent representative of Nasci's compositional skill and characteristic abilities as well as the larger cultivation of instrumental forms in Naples. The careful balance between the soloist and accompaniment underlined by the calculated formal and harmonic architecture, while also requiring rigorous technical abilities for both the soloist and accompaniment, speak to a mature style and command of genre. The choice of a mature sonata form in this movement (and select others) illustrate the continued advance and vibrancy of Neapolitan instrumental music.

A younger contemporary of Nasci, Saverio Chiapparelli's entrance to the Cappella can be traced to sources in the *Tesoreria antica*. Specifically, his admission ties to the notice of a colleague's death. In particular, the document recounts:

> Vacated by the death of the fourth violinist of the Royal Chapel of Naples, Pietro Antonacci, the salary of eight ducats per month, the King has deigned to convey from the aforementioned salary to the first violinist Francesco Lecce an additional six ducats per month [and] to convey the *piazza* of Lecce to Saverio Chiapparelli first supernumerary violinist.[213]

For Chiapparelli, his appointment began a long tenure with the ensemble that continued until the end of the eighteenth and into the early part of the nineteenth century. Similar to his contemporaries, Chiapparelli also maintained a profile as a composer, leaving a small quantity of compositions including an instrumental serenata and sinfonia. The serenata is scored for violins I, II, & III, pairs of oboes, clarinets, horns, cello, and bass.[214] This designation, in the eighteenth century, posited music most often for social occasions, and, as noted in an earlier section, Naples hosted a vibrant social life, especially among the elite classes within the orbit of the court. This also included the frequent private concerts sponsored by Maria Carolina, making this composition appropriate for such an event. Chiapparelli's *serenata* can be allocated into three movements, each with further sectional divisions, distinguished by essential changes in tempo, meter, key, and character. The third movement represents the culmination of this *serenata*, outlining seven individual units with minimal sectional repetition. The essential musical discourse unfolds in the three violin parts as a contrast between the stately Largo sections and the more playful Allegretto units that serve as melodic and rhythmic counterpoints. Each of the Largo segments of the third movement presents a series of melodic strains in cut-time, grounded (for the most part) in the tonic, E-flat major. Nevertheless, these strains unfold as asymmetrical units. For example, the initial Largo spans fifty-five measures that progress as strains of 10, 8, 13, and 24 bars of music respectively. Although the basic phrase unit is two measures, each is subject to extension and/or internal repetition. The three framing Allegretto sections provide contrast in key (for the most part the dominant and secondary dominant tonalities), meter (2/4), and a singular reliance upon the same brisk, running figure for each statement. In contrast, the Largo sections offer an abundance of melodic material (once again as successive asymmetrical strains) to provide

---

[213] *Tesoreria antica*, #79; f. 433r.
[214] Saverio Chiapparelli, *Serenata con obbligazioni di Primo, Secondo, e Terzo Violino, Oboè, Clarinetti, Corni, e Basso del Signore Don Saverio Chiapparelli* (I-Nc: shelf-mark MS 1012–1022; Olim X.2178).

contrast. The winds in the *serenata*, whether the clarinet or oboe, provide a contrast in color and texture. Each group contributes to the essential musical texture, whether through interjecting brief solos or reinforcing the cadential passages. The horns remain relegated to punctuation (as to be expected in light of contemporary performance practices), while the lower strings round out and bolster the harmonic textures. Chiapparelli's *serenata* presents the characteristic features of the instrumental genre: light-hearted, lyrical melodies underpinned by simplistic harmonic progressions. For the most part, the melodic strains resemble those of contemporary social dances, especially the contradance. In particular, the repetitive gestures, the fundamental two-bar phrases shifts in meter (especially from duple to triple) and the profusion of new, successive melodic ideas. Even the asymmetrical organization of the strains finds a connection to the myriad and often irregular movements of the groupings and patterned steps of the contradance. These features distinguish this *serenata* as an ideal accompaniment to the typical social event often entrusted to the Cappella in the private or more public spheres of the Palazzo Reale or any of the *siti reali*.

Maestri da Fiato

The lion's share of attention in scholarship regarding the compositional activities of the *maestri strumentisti* has been justifiably placed upon the string *virtuosi* of the ensemble. The higher professional profile of these artists and greater diffusion of their music has been the basis for this recognition. The membership of the Cappella included a broad range of musicians, who also contributed works for winds, none more prominent than Ferdinando Lizio and Francesco Ricupero. Both of these *maestri* had long tenures with the Cappella and their activities also extended to membership in the orchestra of the San Carlo. Lizio and Ricupero distinguished themselves, moreover, as pedagogues, whether through service to the Neapolitan conservatory system or the composition of didactic compositions designed to benefit the formation of developing musicians. Ricupero achieved a distinguished career within the Cappella and music circles of the capital. Ricupero's composition profile, however, displayed a significantly greater breadth and quantity of surviving music. The first mention of Ricupero stems from records pertaining to the Cappella from both the *Ministero degli affari ecclesiastici* and *Tesoreria antica*. The first source notes, "To Francesco Ricupero, professor of bassoon, who has served for a long time without compensation, ten *carlini* per month."[215] Under the same date, however, listed in the *Tesoreria antica*, he

---

[215] *Ministero degli affari ecclesiastici*, Registro 2; fascio #399; f. 93r.

is cited as "bassoonist of the Royal Chapel with a salary of one ducat per month."[216] By 1779, Ricupero had been admitted to another local ensemble of distinction, cited for "having performed as bassoonist in the Royal Theater of San Carlo."[217] It is evident that his reputation continued to grow in subsequent years as one notice recounts:

> To be paid to Don Francesco Ricupero Maestro di Cappella, one-hundred forty ducats of which should be distributed to the instruments and voices that participated in performing the music in the Church of Our Ladies Cloistered of Santa Patrizia on September 17, [1781] for the profession of vows for my niece Donna Maria Carlotta.[218]

Ricupero's recognition as *maestro di cappella* itself is significant and underlines his growing reputation in the field of composition. The payment specifies that he had led the performance of music for the aforementioned profession of vows, and one can assert that in all likelihood had contributed his own work. Finally, the commission came from Barone Antonio Ricciulli del Fosso, placing the composer within rarified aristocratic circles and the associated network of ceremonial events often requiring the creation of new music. Ricupero's surviving catalogue of music represents a significant body of works numbering in the hundreds, spanning sacred and secular, vocal and instrumental genres, as well as public and private contexts.[219] Within the contemporary holdings of the Biblioteca del Conservatorio San Pietro a Majella resides a collection of autograph manuscripts providing an excellent representation of the composer's music.[220] The contents are exclusively instrumental genres and include sonatas, concertos, and orchestral works. There are also small-scale chamber pieces (primarily duos), and even compositions labeled as didactic works, including contrapuntal exercises as well as some bearing the descriptive label of "studio." Taken altogether, this music demonstrates the breadth and skill of Ricupero.

The *Concerto per flauto traverso con violini, corni da caccia, e basso* (1797) can be viewed as a representative work of the composer.[221] Conceived in the traditional three-movement outline and alternation of fast-slow-fast *tempi*, each is a substantive statement with the finale providing a thrilling close to the concerto. The Allegro finale spans two-hundred seventy-one measures, cast in the tonic G major, and in 2/4 meter. The formal outline of this movement reflects

---

[216] *Tesoreria antica*, # 76; f. 198r. [217] See Di Dato, *et al.*, "Notizie dello Spirito Santo," 883.
[218] See Di Dato, *et al.*, "Notizie dello Spirito Santo," 971. [219] See his works at *opac.sbn.it*.
[220] Francesco Ricupero, *Composizioni didattiche e musicali* (I-Nc: MS 8047–8061).
[221] Francesco Ricupero, *Concerto per flauto traverso con violini, corni da caccia, e basso, 1797* (I-Nc: shelf-mark MS 8050).

Table 8 Outline of Ricupero's *Concerto for Flauto traverso*; Movement III

Measures:			
	1–111	112–164	165–271
Section:			
	Exposition	Development	Recapitulation
Form:			
	Ritornello 1 (mm. 1–46)	Rit. 3 (mm. 112–122)	Rit. 4 (mm. 165–175)
	Episode 1 (mm. 47–65)	Episode 3 (mm. 123–164)	Episode 4 (mm. 176–195)
	Ritornello 2 (mm. 66–71)		Rit. 5 (mm. 195–198)
	Episode 2 (mm. 72–111)		Episode 5 (m. 199–244)
			Rit. 6 (mm. 245–254)
			Cadenza
			Rit. 7 (mm. 255–271)
Key:			
	G major	D; A; B major	G major
Schemata:			
	Triadic ascent		Triadic ascent
	Do-Re-Mi		Do-Re-Mi
	Meyer		Meyer
	Indugio		Indugio
	Mi-Re-Do		Mi-Re-Do
	Prinnner		Prinnner

the characteristic sonata-concerto concept of the late eighteenth century. Table 8 summarizes its formal dimensions.

As illustrated earlier, an evident symmetry emerges in the rendering of the sectional division within the sonata-concerto structure. The lengthy Exposition sets into motion the musical discourse of the concerto with the initial ritornello introducing an assortment of schemata from which the primary thematic material is derived. Musical Example 5 (mm. 1–15) presents the declarative opening of the first ritornello, in which several schemata appear transparently. The opening gesture by the violins presents a nascent Triadic Ascent (over the tonic pedal), which is succeeded by a Do-Re-Mi (mm. 7–8), that flows seamlessly into a Prinner Riposte (mm. 10–11) and rounded off by a closed Meyer (mm. 11–12). The entrance of the soloist overlaps with the prior Meyer schema and immediately offers a reiteration of the Triadic Ascent. The flute's initial gambit (the Triadic Ascent schema) is equally distinguished by a lucid contrapuntal relationship to the preliminary motive of the violins (a rising, sequential third figure; mm. 2–3). In contrast, the soloist presents a falling sequential third figure (mm. 14–15). The reiterated Triadic Ascent upon the entrance of the solo flute (mm. 12–14) is extended with the characteristic 7–2–4 melodic voice leading over the dominant seventh harmony leading (not shown), which leads directly to the cadential prolongation in the form of an Indugio schema (mm. 21–26). The winding down of the first ritornello takes the shape of a broad close (mm. 27–46) in which successive schema (a Mi-Re-Do, succeeded by reiterated Meyer schemas) leads to the expected cadence in the tonic, G major.

Musical Example 5 Francesco Ricupero. *Concerto per flauto traverso con violini, corni da caccia, e basso, 1797.* I-Nc: shelf-mark MS 8050.

Musical Example 5 (cont.)

The first solo Episode (mm. 47–65) establishes an immediate relationship to Ritornello I through its opening Triadic Descent (mm. 47–49), quickly restated in imitation by the first violin (mm. 49–51), which rebounds quickly to form a Triadic Ascent (mm. 51–53). The ensuing passages offer a sequential elaboration of the Triadic Descent before yielding to a pair of successive Prinner Ripostes to bring the initial episode to a close. Ricupero recalls only a brief motive of the Ritornello passage, an appoggiatura-like flourish in the second violin (mm. 66–71) before the soloist begins Episode 2. Preserving the conventional approach, the solo flute offers a Triadic Ascent to begin the second episode, which rapidly modulates through an extension by means of the 7–2–4 melodic voice leading as the secondary dominant pedal tonality (A major) prevails. These passages for the soloist express exposed motivic ideas over a sparse accompaniment, unfolding in the fifth and sixth octaves of the flute's register. There is once again an evident reference to prior melodic material and schemata as Episode 2 winds toward a close, culminating in a confirmation of D major. The ensuing third ritornello initiates the Development portion of the formal structure and as such it preserves the dominant tonality unfolding primarily as a series of Meyer schemata. The repetition of the aforementioned schemata generates a latent tension preparing for the ensuing third solo episode. This section is distinguished by an abundance of idiomatic material for the soloist, recalling both prior melodic ideas and schemata. The opening gesture by the flute, clothed in perfunctory Romanesca and Prinner schemata (mm. 123–128), also recalls earlier material. Of particular importance is the harmonic progression in which the extended dominant pedal (A major) eventually culminates in reiterated dominant-seventh sonorities, concluding on a stunning B-major half-cadence (m. 164). The conclusion of the Development section sets the stage for the reprise of the tonic tonality and associated thematic material, effected in m. 165. Ricupero opts, however, to telescope the recall of prior music within both the fourth ritornello and the fourth episode. These sections remain largely faithful to their presentation earlier in the movement, while also providing tonal stability through the return to G major. The obligatory statement of the fifth ritornello (and the motive in the second violin part) sets the stage for Episode 5, which is surprisingly the longest of the concerto. This section dutifully presents earlier material and the solo flute shines once again in these idiomatic passages. These qualities also posit an emphasis on this section of the structural outline suggesting that the Recapitulation represents culmination rather than a simple reprise. This assertion is bolstered by the looming Cadenza noted in the score. After a brief recall of the ritornello motive, the Cadenza is indicated for the soloist. At its conclusion, the last ritornello provides a fitting end to the movement.

Ricupero's *Concerto for Flute* is an impressive statement of compositional craft as well as contemporary performance practice standards for Neapolitan wind *virtuosi*. The wealth of expressive idiomatic writing and abundance of schemata underscores the provenance of the concerto and Ricupero's training (in all likelihood) in one of the Neapolitan conservatories. Of particular importance is the formal unity and cohesion displayed in the composer's mastery of the sonata-concerto structure. The reliance upon a discreet collection of schemata, especially the prominent utilization of the Triadic Ascent, accentuates and binds together seamlessly the established protocols of formal design. The idiomatic writing for the flute (as well as string accompaniment for that matter) prevails throughout the entirety of the concerto and requires a noteworthy technique and interpretative abilities on the part of the soloist. The bold harmonic underpinning of the finale movement, especially within the Development section, exceeded the customary outline of four accidentals and demonstrates an evident willingness to surpass established norms. Taken altogether, this concerto offers a bold testament to an often-neglected sector of Neapolitan instrumental music and encourages further exploration of Ricupero's contemporaries.

Epilogue

The *virtuosi* of the Cappella, as detailed in the present section, distinguished themselves not only by their practical skills, but also by noteworthy compositional craft. The music studied represents only a small fraction and largely reflects Neapolitan provenance. There is ample evidence that the works of these individuals circulated beyond the Kingdom of Naples, and this fact merits further as well as more detailed study. This research would also expand as well as deepen existing knowledge about the diverse networks of patronage beyond the Bourbon court, especially within aristocratic and diplomatic social circles. It may also lead to greater understanding of how these musicians engaged with the religious institutions and culture of Naples. This inquiry could also shed light on the dense infrastructure of professional associations and how members of the Cappella had been affiliated with virtually every significant local music ensemble. Finally, additional study may even provide biographical details of the musicians of the Cappella, who for the most part have remained overshadowed by the *divi* of the dramatic stage and largely relegated to secondary interest.

Bibliography

Manuscript Sources

Archivio di Stato di Napoli (ASN):
Casa reale Antica, Categorie diverse 343 II/B.
Casa reale Antica, Categorie diverse 343 III.
Casa reale Antica, # 2222–2224.
Casa reale Antica, # 1517 TER.
Ministero degli affari ecclesiastici, Registro 1; volume 5.
Ministero degli affari ecclesiastici, Registro 1; volume 19.
Ministero degli affari ecclesiastici, Registro 1; volume 20.
Ministero degli affari ecclesiastici, Registro 1; volume 25.
Ministero degli affari ecclesiastici, Registro 1; volume 39.
Ministero degli affari ecclesiastici, Registro 1; volume 52.
Ministero degli affari ecclesiastici, Registro 1; volume 67.
Ministero degli affari ecclesiastici, Registro 1; volume 127.
Ministero degli affari ecclesiastici, Registro 1; volume 185.
Ministero degli affari ecclesiastici, Registro 1; volume 192.
Ministero degli affari ecclesiastici, Registro 1; volume 198.
Ministero degli affari ecclesiastici, Registro 1; volume 223.
Ministero degli affari ecclesiastici, Registro 1; volume 266.
Ministero degli affari ecclesiastici, Registro 1; volume 294.
Ministero degli affari ecclesiastici, Registro 1; volume 297.
Ministero degli affari ecclesiastici, Registro 1; volume 301.
Ministero degli affari ecclesiastici, Registro 1; volume 330.
Ministero degli affari ecclesiastici, Registro 1; volume 370.
Ministero degli affari ecclesiastici, Registro 1; volume 372.
Ministero degli affari ecclesiastici, Registro 1; volume 374.
Ministero degli affari ecclesiastici, Registro 1; volume 399.
Ministero degli affari ecclesiastici, Registro 1; volume 419.
Ministero degli affari ecclesiastici, Registro 1; volume 433.
Ministero degli affari ecclesiastici, Registro 1; volume 499.
Ministero degli affari ecclesiastici, Registro 1; volume 509.
Tesoreria antica Scrivania di Razione e Ruota dei Conti, volume 38.
Tesoreria antica Scrivania di Razione e Ruota dei Conti, volume 61.
Tesoreria antica Scrivania di Razione e Ruota dei Conti, volume 67.
Tesoreria antica Scrivania di Razione e Ruota dei Conti, volume 76.
Tesoreria antica Scrivania di Razione e Ruota dei Conti, volume 78.

Tesoreria antica Scrivania di Razione e Ruota dei Conti, volume 79.
Tesoreria antica Scrivania di Razione e Ruota dei Conti, volume 110.
Tesoreria antica Scrivania di Razione e Ruota dei Conti, volume 149.

Catena, Antonio. *Raccolta di diversi Solfeggi per una voce sola di Soprano, e Basso*. Naples: Luigi Marescalchi, s.d. I-Nc, shelf-mark Solfeggio 93; 34.2.9.

Catena, Antonio. *Vorrei l'amaro affanno*. Naples: s.d. I-Nc, shelf-mark 642.11.

Cafaro, Pasquale. *Aria per Vespina/nel secondo atto dell'Opera intitolata/il Marchese Villano*/per/S.M. La Regina/Cafaro 1776. I-Nc, shelf-mark Rari 1.9.22.

Chiapparelli, Saverio. *Serenata con obbligazioni di Primo, Secondo, e Terzo Violino, Oboè, Clarinetti, Corni, e Basso del Signore Don Saverio Chiapparelli*. I-Nc, shelf-mark MS 1012–1022; Olim X.2178.

Composizioni vocali profane, I-Nc, shelf-mark Arie 41.

Lizio, Ferdinando. *Concerto di Fagotto solo con violini, e basso* (1769). I-Nc, shelf-mark MS 5256.

Millico, Giuseppe. *La pietà d'amore. Dramma messo in musica*. Naples: Giuseppe-Maria Porchelli, 1782.

Montoro, Antonio. *Ninna, per il Santissimo Natale, Composizioni vocali sacre*. I-Nc, shelf-mark 21.5.18, 77–136.

Montoro, Antonio. *Sette sinfonie con due violini, due oboi, corni, e basso*. Biblioteca del Conservatorio di Milano Fondo Noseda M 29–9.

Nasci, Michele. *Dieci correnti per violino*. I-Nc, shelf-mark MS 6273; 22.6.19.

Ricupero, Francesco. *Composizioni didattiche e musicali*. I-Nc, MS 8047–8061.

Ricupero, Francesco. *Concerto per flauto traverso con violini, corni da caccia, e basso, 1797*. I- Nc: shelf-mark MS 8050.

Santangelo, Aniello. *Trii*. I-Nc, shelf-mark 34.3.21.

Sinfonie di Cimarosa, Sterckel [sic], *Tritta* [sic], *Cimarosa, Gabellone, Naumann, Schusther* [sic], *e Guglielmi*. I-Nc, shelf-mark MS 66.

Eighteenth-Century Periodicals

Diario Estero
Diario Ordinario
Gazzetta di Napoli
Gazzetta Universale
Notizie del Mondo

Printed Sources

Acton, Harold. *I Borboni di Napoli*. Milan: Martello, 1962.

Ajello, Raffaele. "I filosofi e la regina: il governo delle Due Sicilie da Tanucci a Caracciolo (1776–1786)." *Rivista Storica Italiana* 13 (1991): 398–454, 657–738.

Ajello, Raffaele. "Le Due Sicilie nel secolo XVIII: dalle speranze alla disillusione." In Attilio Antonelli, ed., *Cerimoniale dei Borbone di Napoli 1734–1801*, 17–42.

Albano, Giuliana. "Il Teatro di Corte: appunti d'archivio." In Paologiovanni Maione and Patrizio Di Maggio, eds., *La scena del Re: Il Teatro di Corte*, 90–99.

Algarotti, Francesco. *Saggio sopra l'opera in musica*. Livorno: Marco Coltellini, 1763, 52–55.

Alisio, Giancarlo. "I Siti Reali." In Raffaello Causa, ed., *Civiltà del '700 a Napoli 1734–1799*, vol. I. Florence: Centro di, 1979, 72–105.

Alisio, Giancarlo. *Siti reali dei Borboni: Aspetti dell'architettura napoletana del Settecento*. Rome: Officina, 1976.

Alisio, Giancarlo. *Urbanistica napoletana del Settecento*. Bari: Dedalo, 1979.

Amato, Mauro. "La biblioteca del conservatorio 'San Pietro a Majella' di Napoli: dal nucleo originale alle donazioni di fondi privati ottocenteschi." In Rosa Cafiero and Marina Marino, eds., *Francesco Florimo e l'Ottocento musicale*, vol. II. Reggio Calabria: Jason editrice, 1999, 645–699.

Anonymous. *Indice di tutti i libri, e spartiti di Musica che conservansi nell'Archivio del R[eale] Conservatorio della Pietà de' Torchini* [sic]. Naples, 1801. I-Nc: shelf-mark 54648.

Antonelli, Attilio ed. *Cerimoniale dei Borbone di Napoli 1734–1801*. Naples: Arte'm, 2017.

Astarita, Tommaso. *Between Salt Water and Holy Water: A History of Southern Italy*. New York: W. W. Norton & Co., 2006.

Astuto, Giovanni. "Dalle riforme alle rivoluzioni: Maria Carolina d'Asburgo: una regina austriaca nel Regno di Napoli e di Sicilia." *Quaderni del Dipartimento di Studi Politici* 1 (2007): 27–51.

Avallone, Paola. "The Utilisation of Human Resources in Banking during the Eighteenth Century: The Case of Public Banks in the Kingdom of Naples." *Financial History Review* 6 (October 1999): 111–125.

Battaglini, Mario. *La Repubblica napoletana: origini, nascita, struttura*. Rome: Bonacci, 1992.

Beales, Derek. *Enlightenment and Reform in Eighteenth-Century Europe*. London: I. B. Tauris, 2005.

Bellina, Anna Maria, ed. *Ranieri Calzabigi Scritti teatrali e letterati*. 2 vols. Rome: Editore Salerno, 1994.

Biggi-Parosi, Elena. "Les Danaïdes di Tschudi-Du Roullet e Salieri e i suoi debiti nei confronti di Ipermestra o le Le Danaidi di Calzabigi." In Federico Marri and Francesco Russo, eds., *Ranieri Calzabigi tra Vienna e Napoli*, Atti del convegno di studi (Livorno, September 23–24, 1996). Lucca: LIM, 1998, 101–127.

Bignamini, Ilaria. "The Grand Tour: Open Issues." In Andrew Wilton and Ilaria Bignamini, eds., *Grand Tour: The Lure of Italy*, 31–36.

Blunt, Anthony. "Caratteri dell'architettura napoletana dal tardo barocco al classicismo." In Raffaello Causa, ed., *Civiltà del '700 a Napoli 1734–1799*, 60–71.

Blunt, Anthony. *Architettura barocca e roccocò a Napoli*. Naples: Electa, 2006.

Borelli, Rosaria. *La Lucchesi Palli: storia di una biblioteca napoletana*. Naples: Associazione Voluptuaria, 2010.

Bossa, Renato. "Luigi Vanvitelli spettatore teatrale a Napoli." *Rivista italiana di musicologia* XI (1976): no. 1; 48–70.

Brizi, Bruno. "Uno spunto polemico calzabigiano: Ipermestra e le Danaidi." In Federico Marri, ed., *La figura e l'opera di Ranieri de' Calzabigi*, 119–45.

Buccaro, Alfredo and Gennaro Matacena, eds., *Architettura e urbanistica dell'età borbonica: le opere dello stato, i luoghi dell'industria*. Naples: Electa Napoli, 2004.

Burney, Charles. *The Present State of Music in France and Italy: Or, the Journal of a Tour through Those Countries, Undertaken to Collect Materials for a General History of Music*. London: T. Becket and Co., 1771.

Burney, Charles. *The Present State of Music in Germany, the Netherlands, and United Provinces*, 2nd ed. 2 vols. London: T. Becket, J. Robson, and G. Robinson, 1775.

Burney, Charles. *Music, Men and Manners in France and Italy 1770*. London: Eulenberg, 1974.

Cafiero, Rosa. "Una biblioteca per la biblioteca: la collezione musicale di Giuseppe Sigismondo." In Bianca Maria Antolini and Wolfgang Witzenmann, eds., *Napoli e il teatro musicale in Europa tra Sette e Ottocento: Studi in onore di Friedrich Lippmann*. Florence: Olschki, 1993, 299–367.

Canessa, Francesco. "Il ritorno del Settecento nella Sala Regia." In Paologiovanni Maione and Patrizio Di Maggio, eds., *La scena del Re: Il Teatro di Corte*, 166–175.

Cantone, Gaetana. "Il teatro del re: dalla corte alla città." In Franco Carmelo Greco and Gaetana Cantone, eds., *Il teatro del re*, 43–80.

Cantone, Gaetana. "Ferdinando Fuga." In *Dizionario Biografico degli Italiani*. Vol. 50 (1998), consulted August 9, 2024. www.treccani.it/enciclopedia/ferdinandofuga_%28Dizionario-Biografico%29/.

Caputo, Simone, Franco Piperno, and Emanuele Senici. *Music, Place, and Identity in Italian Urban Soundscapes circa 1850–1860*. New York: Routledge Books, 2023.

Caridi, Giuseppe. *Essere re e non essere re: Carlo di Borbone a Napoli e le attese deluse 1737–1738*. Soveria Mannelli: Rubbettino, 2006.

Caridi, Giuseppe. "Una moglie per l'emancipazione del re: Carlo di Borbone dai progetti nuziali al matrimonio." *Mediterranea* III (2005): 119–148.

Causa, Raffaello, ed. *Civiltà del '700 a Napoli 1734–1799*. 2 vols. Florence: Centro di, 1980.

Cecere, Imma. "L'immagine delle regine di Napoli nel Settecento: Maria Amalia e Maria Carolina." In Mirella Mafrici, ed., *All'ombra della corte*, 191–202.

Celano, Carlo. *Notizie del bello dell'antico e del curioso della città di Napoli. Edizione critica della ristampa del 1792 con le aggiunte del 1724 e del 1758–59*, edited by Gianpasquale Greco. Naples: Rogiosi Editore, 2018, 92; 565–570.

Chierici, Gino. *La Reggia di Caserta*. Rome: La Libreria dello Stato, 1937.

Chiosi, Elvira. "Politica culturale e istituzioni a Napoli nel XVIII secolo." In Attilio Antonelli, ed., *Cerimoniale dei Borbone di Napoli 1734–1801*, 91–108.

Ciapparelli, Pier Luigi. *Due secoli di teatri in Campania 1694–1896: teorie, progetti, e realizzazzioni*. Naples: Electa, 1999.

Ciapparelli, Pier Luigi. "Apparati e scenografia nella Sala Regia." In Gaetana Cantone, ed., *Barocco napoletano*, vol. II, 369–370.

Ciapparelli, Pier Luigi. *Luigi Vanvitelli e il teatro di corte di Caserta*. Naples: Electa Napoli, 1995.

Ciapparelli, Pier Luigi. "I luoghi del Teatro a Napoli nel Seicento. Le sale 'private.'" In Domenico Antonio d'Alessandro and Agostino Ziino, eds., *La musica a Napoli durante il Seicento*. Rome: Edizioni Torre d'Orfeo, 1987, 379–414.

Cioffi, Rosanna. "Al di là di Luigi Vanvitelli: storia e storia dell'arte nella Reggia di Caserta." In Jolanda Capriglione, ed., *Caserta. La storia*. Naples: Paparo, 2000, 83–107.

Cioffi, Rosanna and Giovanna Petrenga, eds. *Casa di Re: La Reggia di Caserta fra storia etutela*. Milan: Skira, 2005.

Cioffi, Rosanna, Luigi Mascilli Migliorini, Aurelio Musi, and Anna Maria Rao, eds. *Le vite di Carlo di Borbone: Napoli, Spagna, e America*. Naples: arte,m, 2019.

Cirillo, Ornella. *Carlo Vanvitelli: Architettura e città nella seconda metà del Settecento*. Florence: Alinea editrice, 2008.

Columbro, Marta and Paologiovanni Maione. *La Cappella Musicale del Tesoro di San Gennarotra Sei e Settecento*. Naples: Turchini Edizione, 2008.

Columbro, Marta and Paologiovanni Maione. *Appunti sull'attività musicale della Cappella tra Sei e Settecento*. Naples: Deputazione della Real Cappella del Tesoro di San Gennaro, 2002.

Corsi, Cesare. "Michele Nasci" in *Dizionario Biografico degli Italiani*, Roma, Istituto dell'Enciclopedia Italiana, volume 77 (2012); online www.treccani.it/enciclopedia/michele-nasci_%28Dizionario-Biografico%29/ (accessed July 27, 2022).

Cotticelli, Francesco. "Dal San Bartolomeo al San Carlo: sull'organizzazione teatrale a Napoli nel primo Settecento." *Ariel* IX/1 (gennaio–aprile 1994): 25–45.

Cotticelli, Francesco and Paologiovanni Maione. "Le carte degli antichi banchi e il panorama musicale e teatrale della Napoli di primo Settecento." *Studi Pergolesiani Pergolesi Studies* 4 (2000): 1–129.

Cotticelli, Francesco and Paologiovanni Maione. "Le carte degli antichi banchi e il panorama musicale e teatrale della Napoli di primo Settecento: 1732–1734." *Studi Pergolesiani Pergolesi Studies* 5 (2006): 21–51.

Cotticelli, Francesco and Paologiovanni Maione. *Onesto divertimento ed allegria de' popoli: Materiali per una storia dello spettacolo a Napoli nel primo Settecento*. Milan: Ricordi, 1996.

Cotticelli, Francesco and Paologiovanni Maione, eds. *Storia della musica e dello spettacolo a Napoli: Il Settecento*, 2 vols. Naples: Turchini edizioni, 2009.

Cotticelli, Francesco and Paologiovanni Maione, eds. *Storia della musica e dello spettacolo a Napoli: Il Seicento*, 2 vols. Naples: Turchini edizioni, 2020.

Cotticelli, Francesco and Paologiovanni Maione. *Le istituzioni musicali a Napoli durante il viceregno austriaco (1707–1734): Materiali inediti sulla Real Cappella ed il Teatro di S. Bartolomeo*. Naples: Luciano editore, 1993.

Croce, Benedetto. *I teatri di Napoli*, 2 vols. Naples: Berisio, 1968.

Croll, Gerhard and Irene Brandenburg. "Millico, Giuseppe." *Grove Music Online. Oxford Music Online*. Oxford University Press, www.oxfordmusiconline.com/subscriber/article/grove/music/18697 (accessed July 18, 2024).

D'Antonio, Paola. *L'opera napoletana di Ferdinando Fuga.* Ph.D. thesis; Università degli studi di Napoli, 1996–1997.

De Brosses, Charles. *Lettres familieres sur l'Italie.* Paris, 1799.

De Filippis, Felice and Ulisse Prota-Giurleo. *Il Teatro di Corte del Palazzo Reale di Napoli.* Napoli, 1952.

DeMarco, Domenico. "Per la storia dell'artigianato a Napoli: una ricca fonte documentale." In *L'artigianato in Campania ieri ed oggi,* ed. Francesco Balletta. Naples: Istituto italiano per la storia delle imprese, 1991, 107.

DeMarco, Domenico and Eduardo Nappi. "Nuovi documenti sulle origini e sui titoli del Banco di Napoli." *Revue Internationale d'Histoire de la Banque* 30–31 (1985), 1–78.

De Nicola, Carlo. *Diario napoletano 1798–1825.* Naples: Società Napoletana di Storia Patria, 1906.

De Seta, Cesare. "Grand Tour: The Lure of Italy in the Eighteenth Century." In Andrew Wilton and Ilaria Bignamini, eds., *Grand Tour: The Lure of Italy in the Eighteenth Century.* London: Tate Gallery Publishing, 1996, 13–19.

De Seta, Cesare. *Architettura ambiente e società a Napoli nel '700.* Torino: Einaudi, 1981.

De Simone, Paola. "Dalla serenata Cerere placata a palazzo Perrelli: Nuovi documenti per le arti a Napoli." In *Ricerche sull'arte a Napoli in età moderna.* Naples: Arte'm, 2015.

De Simone, Paola. "Documenti dell'archivio Farnesiano relativi all'attività teatrale negli anni 1774–78," 269–276.

De Simone, Paola. "La Cerere placata di Niccolò Jommelli: innovazione e interazione fra i diversi linguaggi dell'arte in gioco fra Napoli e l'Europa." In Gaetano Pitaressi, ed., *Niccolò Jommelli, l'esperienza europea di un musicista "filosofo," Atti del Convegno internazionale di Studi (Reggio Calabria, 7–8 ottobre 2011).* Reggio Calabria: Edizioni del Conservatorio di Musica F. Cilea, 2014. Online publication, 457–1054.

DelDonna, Anthony R. "Behind the Scenes." In Maione, *Fonti d'archivio per la storia della musica,* 427–448.

DelDonna, Anthony R. "Beyond the Gilded Stage: Operatic Maestri and Instrumental Music in Late Eighteenth-Century Naples." *Acta Musicologica* 90 (2018): 1–22.

DelDonna, Anthony R. "A Documentary History of the Clarinet in the San Carlo Opera Orchestra in the Late Eighteenth Century." *Studi musicali* 36 (2008): 409–468.

DelDonna, Anthony R. "Eighteenth-Century Politics and Patronage: Musical Practices before and after the Republican Revolution of Naples," *Eighteenth-Century Music* 4 (2007): 211–250.

DelDonna, Anthony R. "Production Practices at the Teatro di San Carlo, Naples, in the Late 18th Century," *Early Music* 30 (2002): 429–445.

DelDonna, Anthony R. "Rinfreschi e composizioni poetiche: the *feste di ballo* tradition in late eighteenth-century Naples." *Eighteenth-Century Studies* 44, no. 2 (2011): 157–188.

DelDonna, Anthony R. "Social Dance, and Spectacle at the Teatro di San Carlo in Late Eighteenth-Century Naples." Rome: Aracne Press, 2020: 125–146.

DelDonna, Anthony R. *Instrumental Music in Late Eighteenth-Century Naples: Politics, Patronage, and Artistic Culture*. Cambridge: Cambridge University Press, 2021.

DelDonna, Anthony R. *Naples, Capital of Dance: The feste di ballo tradition in the Long Eighteenth-Century*. Cambridge: Cambridge University Press, Forthcoming: 2025.

DelDonna, Anthony R. *Opera, Theatrical Culture and Society in Late Eighteenth-Century Naples*. Surrey: Ashgate, 2012.

DelDonna, Anthony R. "Tradition, Innovation, and Experimentation: The dramatic stage and new modes of performance in late eighteenth-century Naples." *Quaderni d'Italianistica*, 36, 1 (2015): 139–172.

Del Puglia, Raffaella. *La regina di Napoli. Il regno di Maria Carolina dal Vesuvio alla Sicilia*. Pavia: Editoriale Viscontea, 1989.

Detroit Institute of Arts. *The Golden Age of Naples: Art and Civilization under the Bourbons, 1734–1805*, exhibition catalogue, Detroit Institute of Arts, August 11–November 1, 1981; Chicago Art Institute, December 24, 1981–March 8, 1982. Detroit: The Detroit Institute of Arts, 1981.

Di Benedetto, Renato. "Music and Enlightenment." In Girolamo Imbruglia, ed., *Naples in the Eighteenth-Century: The Birth and Death of a Nation State*,. Cambridge: Cambridge University Press, 2000, 135–153.

Di Dato, Giulia, Teresa Mautone, Maria Melchionne, and Carmela Petrarca, "Notizie dallo Spirito Santo: la vita musicale a Napoli nelle carte bancarie." In Paologiovanni Maione and Marta Columbro, ed., *Domenico Cimarosa*, 2: 665–1197.

Dietz, Hanns-Bertold. "Instrumental Music at the Court of Ferdinand IV Naples and Sicily and the works of Vincenzo Orgitano." *International Journal of Musicology* 1 (1992): 99–126.

Dietz, Hanns-Bertold. "A Chronology of Maestri and Organisti at the Cappella Reale in Naples, 1745–1800." *Journal of the American Musicological Society* 25 (1972): 379–406.

Di Giacomo, Salvatore. *I quattro antichi conservatorii musicali di Napoli*, 2 vols. Naples: Remo Sandron Editore, 1924.

Di Giacomo, Salvatore. *Il Conservatorio di Sant'Onofrio a Capuana e quello di Santa Maria della Pietà dei Turchini*. Naples: Sandron, 1924.

Di Giacomo, Salvatore. *Maestri di Cappella, Musici ed Istromenti al Tesoro di San Gennaro*. Naples: a spese dell'autore, 1920.

Di Lernia, Luciana. "La visita al San Carlo del viaggiatore straniero." In Franco Carmelo Greco and Gaetana Cantone, *Il teatro del re*, 159–171.

Fabbri, Paolo. "Saverio Mattei: un profilo bio-bibliografico." In Bianca Maria Antolini and Wolfgang Witzenmann, eds., *Napoli e il teatro musicale in Europa tra Sette e Ottocento: Studi in onore di Friedrich Lippmann*. Firenze: Olschki editore, 1993, 121–144.

Fabbri, Paolo. "Vita e funzione di un teatro pubblico e di corte nel Settecento." In *Il Teatro di San Carlo*, vol. 2, 61–76.

Fedi, Maria and Gianluca Stefani. "Iconografia dello spettacolo e Napoli nel Settecento." In Francesco Cotticelli and Paologiovanni Maione, eds., *Storia della musica e dello spettacolo a Napoli: il Settecento*. Vol. I. Naples: Turchini edizioni, 331-412.

Feldman, Marta. *The Castrato: Reflections on Natures and Kinds*. Berkeley: University of California Press, 2016.

Fertonani, Cesare. "Musica strumentale a Napoli durante il Settecento." In Francesco Cotticelli and Paologiovanni Maione, eds., *Storia della musica e dello spettacolo a Napoli: il Settecento*. Naples: Edizioni Turchini, 2009, 925–963.

Fiengo, Giuseppe. *Organizzazione e produzione edilizia a Napoli all'avvento di Carlo di Borbone*. Naples: Edizione Scientifiche Italiane, 1983.

Finscher, Ludwig. "Der Opernsänger als Komponist: Giuseppe Millico und seine Oper La pietà d'amore." In Klaus Hortschansky, ed., *Opernstudien: Anna Amalie Abert zum 65. Geburtstag*. Tutzing, Hand Schneider, 1975, 57–90.

Florimo, Francesco. *La scuola musicale di Napoli e i suoi conservatori*, 4 vols. Naples: Vincenzo Morano, 1880–1883, reprint Bologna: Arnaldo Forni editore, 2002.

Francovich, Carlo. "Storia della massoneria in Italia." *Dalle origini alla Rivoluzione francese. Florence: La nuova Italia, 1974*.

Frigola, Montserrat Moli. "Festeggiamenti reali al San Carlo (1737–1800)." In Franco Carmelo Greco and Gaetana Cantone, eds., *Il teatro del re*, Naples: Edizioni scientifiche, 1987, 173–196.

Galasso, Giuseppe and Rosario Romeo, eds. *Storia del Mezzogiorno*, 15 vols. Naples: Edizioni del Sole, 1991–.

Galasso, Giuseppe, ed. *Storia del Regno di Napoli*, 6 vols. Turin: UTET, 2006.

Galasso, Giuseppe. *Il Regno di Napoli: Il Mezzogiorno borbonico e napoleonico (1734–1815)*. Torino, UTET, 2007.

Galasso, Giuseppe. *Napoli capitale: Identità politica e identità cittadina. Studi e ricerche 1266–1860*. Naples: Electa, 1998.

Gambardella, Alfonso. "Cultura architettonica a Napoli dal viceregno austriaco al 1750." In Gaetana Cantone, ed., *Barocco napoletano*, vol. II. Roma: Istituto Poligrafico e Zecca dello Stato, 1992, 137–155.

Gambardella, Alfonso. *Ferdinando Fuga. 1699–1999 Roma, Napoli, Palermo. Atti del Convegno tenutosi a Napoli nei giorni 25 e 26 ottobre 1999, organizzato dalla Facoltà di Architettura della Seconda Università degli Studi di Napoli*. Naples: Edizioni Scientifiche Italiane, December 2001.

Garella, Luciano, ed. *Carlo. L'utopia di un regno*. Naples: artstudiopaparo, 2016.

Garms-Cornides, Elisabeth. *Cortelazzara: Relazione a Maria Teresa sui Reali di Napoli*. Naples: Franco di Mauro Editore, 1992.

Gasperini, Guido and Franca Gallo. *Catalogo delle opere musicali del Conservatorio di Musica San Pietro a Majella*. Parma, 1934; reprint Bologna: Arnaldo Forni editore, 1988.

Gestal, Pablo Vásquez. "La fondazione del sistema rituale della monarchia delle Due Sicilie (1734–1738)." In Attilio Antonelli, ed., *Cerimoniale dei Borbone di Napoli 1734–1801*, 43–72.

Gestal, Pablo Vásquez. "The System of this Court: Elisabeth Farnese, the Count of Santiesteban, and the Monarchy of the Two Sicilies, 1734–1801." *The Court Historian* 14, 1 (2009): 23–47.

Gialdroni, Giulia. "La musica a Napoli alla fine del XVIII secolo nelle lettere di Norbert Hadrava." *Fonti musicali italiane* 1 (1996): 75–143.

Giarrizzo, Giuseppe. *Massoneria e illuminismo nell'Europa del Settecento*. Venice: Marsilio, 1994.

Gjerdingen, Robert. *Music in the Galant Style*. New York: Oxford University Press, 2007.

Goethe, Johann Wolfgang van. *I miei giorni a Napoli*. Naples: Edizioni Libreria Dante & Descartes, 2016.

Goudie, Allison J. I. "The Sovereignty of the Royal Portrait in Revolutionary and Napoleonic Europe: Five Case Studies Surrounding Maria Carolina, Queen of Naples." DPhil diss., University of Oxford, 2014.

Grazioli, Ulderico. *Origini e sviluppi del sito di Capodimonte in Napoli (il Palazzo Reale, il Bosco, la Fabbrica delle Porcellane*, ed. Ferruccio Diozzi. Naples: Libreria Dante e Descartes, 2020.

Greco, Franco Carmelo and Gaetana Cantone, eds. *Il teatro del re: Il San Carlo da Napoli all'Europa*, 2 vols. Naples: Edizioni scientifiche, 1987.

Griffin, Thomas. *Musical References in the Gazzetta di Napoli 1681–1725*. Berkeley: Fallen Leaf Press, 1993.

Guarino, Gabriel. *Representing the King's Splendour: Communication and Reception of Symbolic Forms of Power in Viceregal Naples (Studies in Early Modern European History)*. New York: Manchester University Press, distributed by Palgrave Macmillan, 2010, 68–101.

Heartz, Daniel. *Music in European Capitals: The Galant Style, 1720–1780*. New York: W. W. Norton & Co., 2003.

Helfert, Joseph Alexander von. *Königin Karolina von Neapel und Sicilien im Kampfe gegen die französische Weltherrschaft (1790–1814)*. Vienna: W. Braumüller, 1878.

Hopkins, Donald R. *The Greatest Killer: Smallpox in History, With a New Introduction*. Chicago: University of Chicago Press, 2002.

Hull, Anthony H. *Charles III and the Revival of Spain*. Washington, DC: University Press of America, 1980.

Imbruglia, Girolamo, ed., *Naples in the Eighteenth Century: The Birth and Death of a Nation State*. Cambridge: Cambridge University Press, 2000.

Kamen, Henry. "Elizabeth Farnese, 1715–1723." In *Philip V of Spain: The King Who Reigned Twice*. New Haven: Yale University Press, 2001, 103–138.

Knight, Carlo. *Hamilton a Napoli: Cultura, svaghi, civiltà di una grande capitale europea*. Naples: Electa Napoli, 2003

Knight, Carlo. *Sulle orme del Grand Tour: uomini, luoghi, società del Regno di Napoli*. Naples: Electa, 1985.

Krause, Ralf. "Documenti per la storia della Real Cappella di Napoli nella prima metà del Settecento." *Annali dell'Istituto italiano per gli studi storici* 11 (1993): 235–257.

Krause, Ralf. "Das musikalische Panorama am neapolitanischen Hofe: zur Real Cappella di Napoli im frühen 18. Jahrhundert" *Analecta Musicologica* 30 (1998): 271–293.

Lancellotti, Carmine. *Elogio di Maria Carolina, Arciduchessa d'Austria, Regina del Regno delle Due Sicilie*. Naples: Tipografia Flautina, 1829.

Le Français de Lalande, Joseph Jérôme. *Voyage d'un François en Italie fait dans les années 1765 & 1766*, vol. 6. Venise: Chez Desaint, Libraire, 1769, 355–356.

Leggi e stabilimenti della Nobile Accademia di Musica delle Signore Dame, e de' Signori Cavalieri nella città di Napoli esistente con Real Permesso de' 7 Maggio 1778. Naples: Filippo Raimondi, 1779.

Lewis, Theresa, ed. *Extracts of the Journals and Correspondence of Miss Mary Berry*, vol. 1. London: Longmans, Green, and Company, 1865.

Lioy, Girolamo. "L'abolizione della Chinea." *Archivio storico per le province napoletane* Anno VII—Fascioli I–IV (1882), 263–92; 497–530; 713–75.

Luigi Vanvitelli e il '700 europeo. Atti del Congresso internazionale di studi, Napoli-Caserta 1973. 2 vols. Naples: Istituto di Storia dell'architettura, Università di Napoli, 1979.

Luongo, Gennaro, ed. *San Gennaro nel XVII centenario del martirio (305–2005)*. 2 vols. Atti del Convegno internazionale Napoli, September 21–23, 2005. Naples: Editoriale Communicazioni Sociali, 2007.

Lynch, John. *Bourbon Spain, 1700–1808*. Oxford: Blackwell Publishers, 1989.

Mafrici, Mirella, ed. *All'ombra della corte: Donne e potere nella Napoli borbonica (1734–1860)*. Naples: Friderciana Editrice Universitaria, 2010.

Mafrici, Mirella. *Il re delle speranze: Carlo di Borbone da Madrid a Napoli*. Naples: Edizioni scientifice italiane, 1998.

Mafrici, Mirella. *Dizionario biografico degli Italiani*, vol. 70 (2008); www.treccani.it/enciclopedia/maria-amalia-di-sassonia-regina-di-napoli-e-sicilia-poi-di-spagna_(Dizionario-Biografico)/.

Magaudda, Ausilia and Danilo Costantini. *Musica e spettacolo nel Regno di Napoli attraverso lo spoglio della Gazzetta 1675–1768*. Rome: Ismez, 2009.

Maione, Paologiovanni and Francesca Seller, eds. *Teatro di San Carlo di Napoli: Cronologia degli spettacoli 1737–1799*, vol. 1. Naples: Altrastampa Edizioni, 2005.

Maione, Paologiovanni and Marta Columbro, eds. *Domenico Cimarosa: Un "napoletano" in europa*, 2 vols. Lucca: Libreria Musicale Italiana, 2004.

Maione, Paologiovanni and Patrizio Di Maggio, eds. *La scena del Re: Il Teatro di Corte del Palazzo Reale di Napoli*. Naples: CLEAN, 2014.

Mancini, Franco, ed. *Il Teatro di San Carlo*, 3 vols. Naples: Electa Napoli 1987.

Mancini, Franco. "La storia, le vicende amministrative, gli organismi di gestione." In Franco Mancini, ed., *Il Teatro di San Carlo*, vol. I, 9–24.

Mancini, Franco. *Le maschere e i carri di Carnevale a Napoli nel periodo barocco*. Naples: Fausto Fiorentino editore, 1963.

Mancini, Franco. "Il San Carlo di Medrano," in *Il Teatro di San Carlo*, vol. 1, 25–88.

Mancini, Franco. *Scenografia napoletana dell'età barocca*. Naples: Edizione Scientifiche Italiane, 1964.

Mancini, Franco. *Feste ed apparati civili e religiosi in Napoli dal Viceregno alla Capitale*. Napoli, Edizione Scientifiche Italiane, 1968.

Manfredi, Tommaso. "Luigi Vanvitelli," *Dizionario Biografico degli Italiani*. Volume 98 (2000): www.treccani.it/enciclopedia/luigi-vanvitelli_%28Dizionario-Biografico%29/.

Marino, John A. *Becoming Neapolitan: Citizen Culture in Baroque Naples*. Baltimore: Johns Hopkins, 2010, 64–116.

Marino, Marina. "Le carte degli antichi banchi e il panorama musicale e teatrale della Napoli di primo Settecento." *Studi pergolesiani/Pergolesi Studies* (2015): 660–677.

Martin, Alison E. and Susan Pickford, eds. *Travel Narratives in Translation, 1750–1830: Nationalism, Ideology, Gender*. New York: Routledge, 2012.

Martina, Alessandra. *Orfeo-Orphée di Gluck: Storia della trasmissione e della recezione*. Torino: Passigli Editori, 1995. 118–127.

Mattei, Saverio. *Per la biblioteca musica fondata nel Conservatorio della Pietà con Reale approvazione. Memoria*. Napoli, 1795.

McClymonds, Marita Petzoldt. "Calzabigi and Paisiello's Elfrida and Elvira: Crumbling Conventions within a Rapidly Changing Genre." In Federico Marri and Francesco Russo, eds., *Ranieri Calzabigi tra Vienna e Napoli*, Atti del convegno di studi (Livorno, September 23–24, 1996) Lucca: Libreria Musicale Italiana, 1998, 239–258.

McClymonds, Marita Petzoldt. "The Italian Opera Sinfonia 1720 to 1800." In *The Symphonic Repertoire, Vol. I: The Eighteenth-Century Symphony*. Bloomington: Indiana University Press, 2012, 117–169.

Mincuzzi, Rosa, ed. *Lettere di Bernardo Tanucci a Carlo III di Borbone (1759–1776)*. Rome: Istituto per la Storia del Risorgimento Italiano, 1969.

Mondolfi Bossarelli, Anna. "Gluck e i contemporanei attraverso i manoscritti donati da Maria Carolina alla città di Napoli." *Chigiana: Rassegna annuale di studi musicologi* IX–X (1975), 585–592.

Montroni, Giovanni. "The Court: Power and Social Life." In *Naples in the Eighteenth Century: The Birth and Death of a Nation State*, 38–39.

Morrison, Alfred, ed. *The Hamilton and Nelson Papers*, 2 vols. London: Printed for Private Circulation, 1892–4.

Morrow, Mary Sue and Bathia Churgin, eds. *The Symphonic Repertoire, Vol. I: The Eighteenth-Century Symphony*. Bloomington: Indiana University Press, 2012, 1–39, 411–471.

Nappi, Eduardo. "Antiche feste napoletane." In *Ricerche sul '600 napoletano: Saggi e documenti 2001*. Naples: Electa, 2002, 76–90.

Nasci, Michele. *Sonate sei di Cembalo con Accompagnamento di Violino*. London: Welcker, 1771.

Nicolini, Fausto. "I banchi pubblici napoletani e i loro archivi." In *Bollettino dell'Archivio Storico del Banco di Napoli I*, 1950, 1–36.

Nicolini, Fausto. *L'Archivio Storico del Banco di Napoli: Una fonte preziosa per la storia economica, sociale, artistica del Mezzo giorno d'Italia*. Naples: L'Arte Tipografica, 1972.

Nicolini, Luigi. *La Reggia di Caserta (1750–1775)*. Bari: Giuseppe Laterza e figli, 1911.

Noel, Charles C. and Clarissa Campbell-Orr, eds. "'Bárbara Succeeds Elizabeth ... ': The Feminisation and Domestication of Politics in the Spanish Monarchy, 1701–1759." In *Queenship in Europe 1660–1815: The Role of the Consort*. Cambridge, Cambridge University Press, 2004, 155–185.

Nuzzo, Giuseppe. *La monarchia delle Due Sicilie tra Ancien Régime e rivoluzione*. Naples: A. Berisio, 1962.

Olivieri, Guido. *String virtuosi in Eighteenth-Century Naples: Culture, Power, and Music Institutions*. Cambridge: Cambridge University Press, 2024.

Olivieri, Guido, "La musica strumentale a Napoli." In Francesco Cotticelli and Paologiovanni Maione, eds., *Storia della musica e dello spettacolo a Napoli: Il Seicento*. Naples: Turchini edizioni, 2020, 1493–1535.

Olivieri, Guido. "Condizione sociale dei musicisti nella Napoli del '700." In Pierpaolo DeMartino, ed., *Napoli Musicalissima: Studi in onore del 70.mo compleanno di Renato Di Benedetto*. Lucca: LIM, 2006, 45-68.

Olivieri, Guido, ed. *Marchitelli, Mascitti e la musica strumentale napoletana fra Sei e Settecento*. Lucca: LIM, 2023.

Padoan, Maurizio. "Music, Language and Society in Antonio Planelli." *International Review of the Aesthetics and Sociology of Music* 19, no. 2 (December 1988), 161–179.

Papagna, Elena. "Cerimoniale e cerimonie di corte nel Settecento napoletano." In Attilio Antonelli, ed., *Cerimoniale dei Borbone di Napoli 1734–1801*, 109–126.

Pascuzzi, Antonella. *Feste e spettacoli di corte nella Caserta del Settecento*. Florence: Firenze libri, 1995.

Passariello, Raffaella and Stefania Prisco. "Le fonti bancarie napoletane sullo spettacolo." In Maria Ida Biggi, Francesco Cotticelli, Paologiovanni Maione, and Iskrena Yordanova, eds., *Le stagioni di Niccolò Jommelli*. Naples: Turchini Edizioni, 2018.

Petrie, Charles. *King Charles III of Spain: An Enlightened Despot*. London: Constable, 1971.

Piozzi, Hester Lynch. *Observations and Reflections Made in the Course of a Journey Through France, Italy, and Germany*, vol. 2. London: A. Strahan and T. Cadell, 1789.

Planelli, Antonio, *Dell'opera in musica*. Naples: Stamperia di Campo, 1772; modern edition by Francesco Degrada, Fiesole: Discanto edizioni, 1981.

Prota-Giurleo, Ulisse. *La grande orchestra del R. Teatro San Carlo nel Settecento*. Naples, 1927.

Prota-Giurleo, Ulisse. "Breve storia del Teatro di Corte e della musica a Napoli nei secoli XVII–XVIII." In Felice De Filippis and Ulisse Prota-Giurleo, eds., *Il Teatro di Corte del Palazzo Reale di Napoli*. Naples: L'Arte Tipografica, 1952, 19–146.

Prota-Giurleo, Ulisse. *I teatri di Napoli nel secolo XVII*, ed. Ermanno Bellucci and Giorgio Mancini. 3 vols. Naples: Il quartiere, 2002.

Rao, Anna Maria. "Corte e Paese: il Regno di Napoli dal 1734 al 1806." In Mirella Mafrici, ed., *All'ombra della corte: Donne e potere nella Napoli borbonica (1734–1860)*. Naples: Friderciana Editrice Universitaria, 2010, 11–30.

Rak, Michele. *Napoli civile: Il popolo civile, la Parte di Popolo e le loro arti in Napoli barocca*. Lecce: Argo, 2021.

Recca, Cinzia, ed. *The Diary of Queen Maria Carolina of Naples, 1781–1785: New Evidence of Queenship at Court*. Basingstoke: Palgrave Macmillan, 2017.

Recca, Cinzia, ed. *Sentimenti e politica: Il diario inedito della regina Maria Carolina di Napoli (1781–1785)*. Milan: Franco Angeli, 2014.

Recca, Cinzia. "Maria Carolina and Marie Antoinette: Sisters and Queens in the Mirror of Jacobin Public Opinion." *Royal Studies Journal* 1 (2014): 17–36.

Recca, Cinzia. "Queenship and Family Dynamics through the Correspondence of Queen Maria Carolina of Naples." In Elena Woodacre, ed., *Mediterranean Queenship: Negotiating the Role of the Queen in the Medieval and Early Modern Eras*. New York: Palgrave Macmillan, 2013, 265–286.

Reumont, Alfred von. *Maria Carolina, regina delle Due Sicilie e i suoi tempi*. Florence: Coi tipi di M. Cellini e C., 1878.

Rice, John. *Empress Marie Therese and Music at the Viennese Court, 1792–1807*. Cambridge: Cambridge University Press, 2003.

Richard, Jean Claude, Abbé de Saint-Non. *Voyage pittoresque ou description des royaumes de Naples et de Sicile*. Paris: de l'Imprimerie de Clousier, 1781–6.

Riggs, Lady Anna Miller. *Letters from Italy, Describing the Manners, Customs, Antiquities, Paintings, &c. of That Country, in the year MDCCLXX and MDCCLXXI*. London: Printed for E. and C. Dilly, 1777.

Robinson, Michael. "A Late Eighteenth-Century Account Book of the San Carlo Theatre, Naples." *Early Music* 18 (1990), 73–82.

Roscioni, Carlo Marinelli, ed. *Il Teatro di San Carlo. La cronologia, 1737–1987*, 2 vols. Naples: Guida editori, 1987.

Rossi, Nicola. *Narrazione delle solenni reali feste fatte celebrare in Napoli da S.[ua] M. [aestà] il Re delle Due Sicilie Carlo Infante di Spagna ecc. Per la nascita del Suo Primogenito Filippo, ecc*. Napoli, 1749.

Sartori, Claudio. *I libretti italiani a stampa dalle origini al 1800*. 6 vols. Turin: Bertola & Locatelli, Cuneo, 1993.

Schipa, Michelangelo. *Nel regno di Ferdinando IV di Borbone*. Florence: Vallecchi editore, 1938.

Sharp, Samuel. *Letters from Italy describing the customs and manner of that country in the years 1765 and 1766*, 3rd edition. London: St. John's Gate, n.d.

Signorelli, Pietro Napoli. *Vicende della cultura delle Due Sicile*, vol. 7. Naples: Vincenzo Flauto, 1811, 3.

Sigismondo, Giuseppe. *Apotheosis of Music in the Kingdom of Naples*, ed. Claudio Bacciagaluppi, Giulia Giovani, and Raffaele Mellace, trans. Beatrice Scaldini, with an introduction by Rosa Cafiero. Rome: Società editrice di musicologia, 2016.

Simioni, Attilio. "Nell'intimità di una reggia: lettere di Ferdinando IV di Napoli a Carlo III di Spagna." Rassegna storica del Risorgimento 11 (1924): 46–67.

Sodano, Giulio and Giulio Brevetti, eds. *Io, la regina. Maria Carolina d'Asburgo-Lorena tra politica, fede, arte e cultura, Quaderni* 33. Palermo: Mediterranea – ricerche storiche 2016.

Spinosa, Nicola, ed. *I Borbone di Napoli*. Naples: Franco di Mauro Editore, 2009.

Spinosa, Nicola. *Capodimonte*. Naples: Electa, 1999.

Spinosa, Nicola. *Alla corte di Vanvitelli: I Borbone e le arti alla Reggia di Caserta*, exhibition catalog, Caserta, Palazzo Reale, April 4–July 6, 2009. Milan: Electa, 2009.

Spitzer, John and Neal Zaslaw. *The birth of the orchestra: history of an institution, 1650–1815*. Oxford: Oxford University Press, 2004.

Stein, Stanley J. and Barbara H. Stein, *Apogee of Empire: Spain and New Spain in the Age of Charles III, 1759–1789*. Baltimore, MD: Johns Hopkins University Press, 2003.

Stiffoni, Gian Giacomo. "Il Teatro di San Carlo dal 1747 al 1753." In Paologiovanni Maione, ed., *Fonti d'archivio per la storia della musica e dello spettacolo a Napoli tra XVI e XVIII secolo*. Naples: Editoriale Scientifica, 2001, 271–374.

Stollberg-Rilinger, Barbara. *Maria Theresa: The Habsburg Empress in Her Time*. Princeton University Press, 2022.

Strazullo, Franco. *Edilizia e urbanistica a Napoli '500 al '700*. Naples: Berisio, 1969.

Strazzullo, Franco. *La Real Cappella del Tesoro di S. Gennaro. Documenti Inediti*. Naples: Società Editrice Napoletana, 1978.

Swinburne, Henry. *Travels in the Two Sicilies, 1777–1780*, vol. 2. London: P. Elmsly, 1783.

Tresoldi, Lucia. *La biblioteca privata di Maria Carolina d'Austria regina di Napoli: Cenni storici*. Rome: Bulzoni, 1972.

Trifone, Romualdo. *Un carnevale alla Corte di Carlo di Borbone*. Salerno: Tipografa Cavaliere A. Volpe & compagnia, 1912.

Tufano, Lucio. "Dall'ascesa al trono di Ferdinando IV alla prima Restaurazione borbonica." In *La scena del Re: Il Teatro di Corte*, 142–147.

Tufano, Lucio. "Opera, Ball and Spoken Theatre at the Royal Palace of Caserta." In Silke Leopold and and Bärbel Pelker, eds., *Fürstliches Arkadien: Sommerresidenzen im 18. Jahrhundert*. Heidelberg: Heidelberg University Publishing, 2021, 129–173.

Tufano, Lucio. "L'orchestra del Teatro San Carlo nel 1780 e nel 1796." In Paologiovanni Maione, ed., *Fonti d'archivio per la storia della musica e dello spettacolo a Napoli tra XVI e XVIII secolo*. Naples: Editoriale Scientifica, 2001, 449–476.

Tufano, Lucio. "Musica, ballo e gioco a Napoli nella seconda metà del Settecento: l'Accademia dei Cavalieri e la Conversazione degli amici..." In Beatrice Alfonzetti and Roberta Turchi, eds., *Spazi e tempi del gioco nel Settecento* (Rome: Edizioni di Storia e Letteratura, 2011), 378–399.

Tufano, Lucio. "Accademie musicali a Napoli nella seconda metà del Settecento: sedi, spazii, e funzioni." In *Quaderni dell'archivio storico*. Naples: Istituto Banco di Napoli, 2005–2006, 113–178.

Tufano, Lucio. "Ancora sull'Accademia dei Cavalieri e la Conversazione degli Amici: Aggiunte e Precisazioni." In *Quaderni dell'archivio storico*. Naples: Istituto Banco di Napoli, 2007–2008, 339–360.

Tufano, Lucio. "Partenope consolata: Rivoluzione e reazione nelle cantate celebrative per il ritorno degli Borboni a Napoli (1799–1802)." *Studi settecenteschi* 19 (1999), 293–342.

Tufano, Lucio. "Una sconosciuta cantata encomiastica di Calzabigi e Millico per Gustavo III di Svezia: Gli Elisi o sia L'ombre degli Eroi." In Federico Marri and Francesco Paolo Russo, eds., *Ranieri Calzabigi tra Vienna e Napoli*, Atti del convegno di studi (Livorno, September 23–24, 1996). Lucca: Libreria Musicale Italiana, 1998, 165–207.

Valsecchi, Franco. *Il riformismo borbonico in Italia*. Rome: Bonacci, 1990.

Vanvitelli, Luigi. *Dichiarazione dei Disegni del Reale Palazzo di Caserta alle Sacre Reali Maestà di Carlo Re delle Due Sicilie e di Gerusalemme: Infante di Spagna, Duca di Parma e di Piacenza. Gran Prencipe Ereditario di Toscana e di Maria Amalia di Sassonia Regina &c &c*. Naples: Regia Stamperia, 1756.

Verdile, Nadia. *Un anno di lettere coniugali: Da Caserta, il carteggio inedito di Ferdinando IV e Maria Carolina*. Caserta: Edizioni spring, 2008.

Verdile, Nadia. "Maria Carolina e la Colonia di San Leucio." In Mirella Mafrici, ed., *All'ombra della corte*, 83–95.

Verdile, Nadia. *L'utopia di Carolina: Il codice delle leggi leuciane*. Naples: Regione Campania, 2007.

Yamada, Takasi. "L'attività e la strategia di Gennaro Blanchi, impresario dei teatri napoletani nella seconda metà del Settecento: Interpretazione del suo sistema di gestione dalle scritture dell'Archivio Storico dell'Istituto Banco di Napoli-Fondazione." In *Quaderni dell'archivio storico* (Naples: Istituto Banco di Napoli Fondazione, 2004), 95–133.

Zecca Laterza, Agostina. "Manuscript Music Published in Naples, 1780–1820." *Fontes Artis Musicae* (April–June 2012): vol. 59, no. 2, 149–157.

Acknowledgments

There are many individuals and institutions to thank for the completion of this project. Georgetown University provided significant financial assistance through the Thomas E. Caestecker Endowed Chair. My colleagues in Naples encouraged this work, especially Guido Olivieri, Paologiovanni Maione, Francesca Seller, Francesco Cotticelli, Cesare Corsi, and Luigi Guerriero. The excellent staff at the Archivio di Stato di Napoli, especially Armando Traglia, provided constant support and help. Mark Janello and Sean Curtice expertly proofed the musical examples. My wife Tina and daughter Alessandra encouraged me at every step and supported my long stays in Naples. I dedicate this project to them for their love and constancy.

Cambridge Elements ≡

Music and Musicians, 1750–1850

Simon P. Keefe
University of Sheffield
Simon P. Keefe is James Rossiter Hoyle Chair of Music at the University of Sheffield. He is the author of four books on Mozart, including *Mozart in Vienna: the Final Decade* (Cambridge University Press, 2017) and *Mozart's Requiem: Reception, Work, Completion* (Cambridge University Press, 2012), which won the Marjorie Weston Emerson Award from the Mozart Society of America. He is also the editor of seven volumes for Cambridge University Press, including *Mozart Studies* and *Mozart Studies 2*. In 2005 he was elected a life member of the Academy for Mozart Research at the International Mozart Foundation in Salzburg.

About the Series

Music and Musicians, 1750–1850 explores musical culture in the late eighteenth and early nineteenth centuries through individual, cutting-edge studies (c. 30,000 words) that imaginatively re-think a period traditionally associated with high classicism and early. The series interrogates images and reputations, composers, instruments and performers, critical and aesthetic ideas, travel and migration, and music and social upheaval (including wars and conflicts), thereby demonstrating the cultural vibrancy of the period. Through discussion of musicians' interactions with one another and with non-musicians, real-world experiences in and outside music, evolving reputations, and little studied career contexts and environments, Music and Musicians, 1750–1850 works across the conventional 'silos' of composer, genre, style, and place, as well as in many instances across the (notional) 1800 divide. All contributions appeal to a wide readership of scholars, students, practitioners and informed musical public.

Cambridge Elements

Music and Musicians, 1750–1850

Elements in the Series

Dr. Charles Burney and the Organ
Pierre Dubois

Bach, Handel and Scarlatti: Reception in Britain 1750–1850
Mark Kroll

The Age of Musical Arrangements in Europe, 1780–1830
Nancy November

Mendelssohn and the Genesis of the Protestant A Cappella Movement
Siegwart Reichwald

The Aesthetic System of François Delsarte and Richard Wagner: Catholicism, Romanticism, and Ancient Music
Bradley Hoover

The Orchestra of the Cappella Reale, Naples, 1750–1800
Anthony R. DelDonna

A full series listing is available at: www.cambridge.org/EIMM

For EU product safety concerns, contact us at Calle de José Abascal, 56–1º,
28003 Madrid, Spain or eugpsr@cambridge.org.

www.ingramcontent.com/pod-product-compliance
Lightning Source LLC
LaVergne TN
LVHW020349260326
834688LV00045B/1613